KOHIMA
1944

KOHIMA
1944

CHRIS BROWN, *1967*

First published 2013 by
Spellmount, an imprint of
The History Press
The Mill, Brimscombe Port
Stroud, Gloucestershire, GL5 2QG
www.thehistorypress.co.uk

© The History Press, 2013

The right of Chris Brown to be identified as the Author
of this work has been asserted in accordance with the
Copyrights, Designs and Patents Act 1988.

British Library Cataloguing in Publication Data.
A catalogue record for this book is available from the British Library.

ISBN 978 0 7524 9141 7

Typesetting and origination by The History Press
Printed in Great Britain

CONTENTS

ACKNOWLEDGEMENTS

I am, as ever, indebted to my wife Pat and to my children for putting up with my interminable ramblings about this little book – and every other book that I have written – and to my editor at The History Press, Jo de Vries, for her advice and patience.

I am particularly grateful to the team at '*Dekko*', the newsletter of the Burma Star Association, who kindly printed an appeal for help which brought me into touch with Mrs Rhona Palmer and Mrs Angela Benions. Mrs Palmer provided me with a copy of her father's memoir of the war in Burma and has generously allowed me to include several photographs from his collection. Mrs Benions very kindly lent me a copy of her father's recollections of the Burma theatre when I failed to find one myself.

I would also like to draw attention to the work of the Kohima Educational Trust. When the veterans of the battle held their last reunion in 2004, they decided to set up a trust to provide assistance with the education of Naga children in memory of the Commonwealth troops who fell in battle, and as an expression of gratitude for the sacrifice and loyalty of the Naga people in whose land the battle was fought. The trust does remarkable and valuable work, and is a cause worthy of support; it can be contacted at www.kohimaeducationaltrust.net.

This book is dedicated to three 'gentlemen gunners' who served their country in the Second World War: my father, Peter Brown, who had the good fortune to arrive at the Burmese border at the best possible juncture of the campaign; to my late father-in-law, Robert Smith, who served in North Africa and Italy; and to John Laindon Cornwell, who was murdered by the Japanese Army on Ballali Island in 1943.

LIST OF ILLUSTRATIONS

12 General Slim. (Author's collection)

13 Gurkhas advancing with tanks to clear the Japanese from the Imphal-Kohima Road in North Eastern British India. (Author's collection)

14 Japanese anti-tank rifle. Virtually ineffective against the later models of Commonwealth tanks, the anti-tank rifle was still a potent weapon against Bren Carriers and armoured cars. (Author's collection)

15 Japanese flag. (Author's collection)

16 A typical Japanese soldier. (Author's collection)

17 Riflemen with the Arisaka rifle. (Author's collection)

18 A speeding Ha-Go Type 95 tank. (Author's collection)

19 The Japanese knee mortar grenade launcher. (Author's collection)

20 A convoy approaching Kohima. (AB/AWH)

21 A convoy on the Kohima Road. (AB/AWH)

22 A landslide blocking the road – a common event in Burma. (AB/AWH)

23 Crossing the Irrawaddy River. (AB/AWH)

24 Loading a pack howitzer onto a raft for a river crossing. (AB/AWH)

25 Commonwealth troops in action in the Arakan. (AB/AWH)

26 American supply trucks on the Burma Road. (AB/AWH)

27 A captured Japanese artillery piece. (AB/AWH)

28 A dug-out at Kohima. (AB/AWH)

29 Defoliation from shelling at Kohima. (AB/AWH)

30 Extensive air supply operations occurred throughout Burma. (AB/AWH)

31 Shattered houses on the Kohima battlefield. (AB/AWH)

32 Commonwealth troops on the march. (AB/AWH)

33 Commonwealth troops manning a light anti-tank gun. (AB/AWH)

34 Airstrike on a Japanese supply train. (AB/AWH)

35 A Fourteenth Army observation post directing artillery fire. (AB/AWH)

Maps

INTRODUCTION

Operation U-Go: the Road to Kohima

The battle, or more accurately, the siege and relief of the Burmese hill town of Kohima is a tale of incredible endurance and collective courage. Although usually associated with one British rifle battalion – 4th Royal West Kents (RWK) – elements of many other regiments, corps and departments were involved; in fact, the majority of the combat soldiers in the garrison comprised Ghurkha, Indian, Nepalese and Burmese soldiers whose service has been rather forgotten.

Although the Japanese attack would eventually fail, it is all too easy to overlook the incredible feat of soldiering involved in bringing a whole division with artillery, engineering and medical assets through many miles of crude tracks, steep mountains, thick forests and dense jungle of western Burma and north-east India. The 31st Division of the Imperial Japanese Army made the march from the Chindwin to Kohima with virtually no motor transport, so General (Gen.) Kotoku Sato's plans largely depended on what his men could carry on their backs, plus trains of mules, ponies, horses and elephants. His force also had no air support, a very limited capacity for dealing with casualties and very poor lines

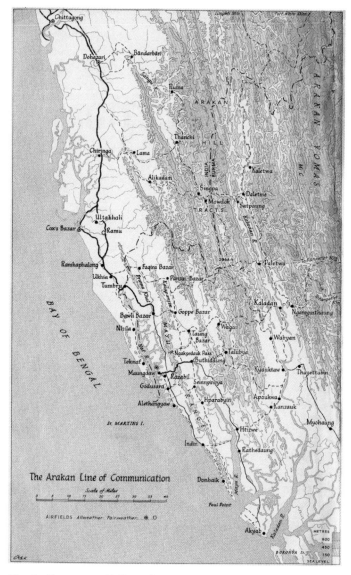

Map 1 *Commonwealth lines of communication in the Arakan. (Butler, James,* The War Against Japan, *p.5)*

of communication. Despite the assurances of his superior, Gen. Renya Mutaguchi, it proved impossible to achieve a reliable line of supply and, although his force attempted to drive large herds of cattle to provide beef on the hoof, his men were soon challenged by hunger, the terrain and an increasingly competent and confident Commonwealth army.

Unlike the Allies, 31st Division was unable to receive supplies by airdrop due to the lack of transport aircraft and the fact that the Royal Air Force (RAF) and the Royal Indian Air Force (RIAF) had, by this time, achieved air superiority. The further the Japanese penetrated into India, the longer their lines of communication; so much so that the planning actually relied on the anticipated capture of supplies from the Allied forces. Although this was a rather optimistic assessment of the situation, it was not totally irrational. The experience of the campaigns in Malaya and Burma had led Japanese staff planners to believe that Commonwealth troops were, at best, brittle in the face of a determined attack and could be driven backwards at great speed, abandoning huge quantities of equipment and stores as they went.

Even so, the Japanese were aware that the Allies were steadily becoming more proficient at living in the jungle, and were also becoming more capable and confident on the battlefield. It was also abundantly clear that the war in general was not going well.

If the huge Pacific perimeter that had been seized in the opening phases of the war against the Commonwealth and the United States was to be held, and if the war in China was to be brought to a favourable conclusion, it was highly desira dble – in fact vital – to knock Britain out of the Asian war completely. To achieve this, the Japanese Army had to obtain a victory on the scale of the Malaya campaign of 1942 and the first Burma campaign that had followed it. If such a victory could be gained, and if the Commonwealth forces in Burma could be utterly destroyed, it was assumed – perhaps correctly – that British prestige in India would be so totally undermined that it would be impossible to raise enough troops or gather sufficient material to form a new army capable of preventing Japanese expansion into north-east India. They thought it was inconceivable that Britain herself could provide a new army for the re-conquest of Burma, given her extensive commitments in Africa, Italy and the imminent invasion of Europe. Even if such a force could be found, the transport demands of the Atlantic and Mediterranean theatres would prevent it from being deployed to Asia or being supplied with the tools for the job.

If such a victory could be brought about, then there would be implications for another theatre of operations: China. By 1944 the stream of war materials to Chiang Kai-shek's armies had steadily increased, and assistance from Britain and the United States in the training of soldiers had improved the quality of the Chinese formations. Breaking the logistic chain would not necessarily force Chiang Kai-shek to abandon the struggle immediately, but there was a possibility that the internal threat from Mao Zedong's communists, coupled with the reduction in supplies, might force China to agree to an armistice or, at the very least, reduce their capacity for offensive operations.

In addition to these factors, there was another, more serious issue facing Japan: her chief ally, Germany, was clearly losing her war against the Soviet Union. Although Stalin was committed to the defeat of the Nazis as his prime objective, he was also committed to the defeat of Japan. The brief Russo-Japanese conflict of the summer of 1939 had been an ignominious experience for Emperor Hirohito's forces, but there was a possibility that forcing the British out of the Asia theatre might encourage Stalin to abandon any thoughts of pursuing the war with Japan once Germany had been defeated.

The campaign in the Pacific was a more pressing matter. Realistically, it is very unlikely that even total success in Burma – which would allow redeployment of resources to the Pacific and reduce strain on the economy – would have given Japan sufficient power to resist the American and Australian forces in the Pacific; however, this may not have been fully grasped in Japanese Government circles. In practice the United States was utterly determined to defeat Japan due to public pressure after Pearl Harbor. The policy of defeating Germany first would undoubtedly have been pursued regardless, but America was not going to give up her plans for recovering her position in Asia and the utter defeat of Japan once Victory in Europe (VE) was achieved. By the summer of 1944 this was clearly on the cards.

Operation U-Go was a tremendous gamble and the odds were even less in favour of a Japanese victory than was apparent to the commanders in Burma – Generals Mutaguchi and Masakazu Kawabe – or to the prime minister, Gen. Hideki Tojo. Equally it is not clear that any other course of action would have been much better. The Japanese Government was aware that the odds were gradually, but steadily, tipping in favour of the Allies in every theatre. If they chose to adopt a defensive policy in Burma then the Allies would eventually gain the initiative and be able to choose the time and place of their offensives, and Japan could not possibly find the men or material to defend the entirety of the Burma-India border in addition to her commitments in China and the Pacific. The chances of victory in Burma were slim, but it was still the only possible route for turning the course of the war in 1944.

TIMELINE

1937	Burma granted autonomy as a separate state from British India, though this was not enough to satisfy the growing Burmese desire for independence
1942	Japanese invasion of Burma
1943	Commonwealth forces mount their first Arakan offensive; Gen. Mutaguchi starts pressing for an offensive toward and into India
1944	**January**	Launch of the Ha-Go offensive in the Arakan to tie down Commonwealth forces ahead of the main U-Go offensive against Commonwealth IV Corps at Imphal. Orders were also given for an attack by Gen. Sato's 31st Division to advance toward Kohima to cut the Dimapur to Imphal road
	8 March	Japanese 33rd Division commences the march on Tiddim
	15 March	Japanese 31st Division crosses the River Chindwin

Timeline

	19 March	Elements of 31st Division encounter resistance from 50th (Indian) Brigade under Brigadier (Brig.) Hope-Thompson at Sheldon's Corner
	21 March	Brigadier Hope-Thompson concentrates his brigade at Sangshak to block – or at least impede – the advance of 31st Division
	22 March	General William Slim starts to form a force to hold the Imphal-Kohima area
	26 March	50th Parachute Brigade withdraws from Sangshak
	27 March	31st Division renews its march on Kohima
	29 March	Imphal comes under air attack and Japanese troops cut the road between Dimapur and Imphal
1944	**3 April**	4th Battalion RWK, 161st Brigade arrive at Kohima only to be ordered to move to Dimapur
	4 April	Leading elements of 31st Division engage at Kohima
	5 April	RWK return to Kohima to find that the town is already under attack
	6 April	The first properly coordinated Japanese attacks on the town of Kohima make considerable progress, but fail to completely cut communications with the balance of 161st Brigade at Jotsoma
	8 April	Elements of Japanese 138th Infantry Regiment separate Jotsoma from Kohima. General Mutaguchi orders 138th Infantry Regiment to proceed to Dimapur
	10 April	Monsoon rains arrive two to three weeks earlier than normal, impeding both Japanese and Commonwealth troop movements and re-supply. The Kohima garrison gives up DIS (Daily Issue Supply) Hill as untenable

1944

17 April FSD Hill and Kuki Piquet taken by the Japanese, severely reducing the perimeter held by Commonwealth forces

20 April Leading elements of 2nd Division force their way through the Japanese lines and into Kohima

23 April General Sato orders a final assault on the remaining Commonwealth strongpoint, Garrison Hill. The attack fails and Sato decides it is time to adopt a defensive posture to prevent Commonwealth forces gaining full use of the road to Imphal

25–29 April 2nd Division completes the relief of the Kohima garrison and mounts extensive flanking movements as part of a series of operations to contain and destroy the Japanese 31st Division

HISTORICAL BACKGROUND

Archaeological evidence indicates that there was widespread human settlement in Burma by about 11,000 BC, but the first recorded population consisted of the Pyu people who migrated into Burma from China about 2,200 years ago and who had developed a sophisticated community of city-states before AD 400, and by the Mon people who settled along the southern coast. In the ninth century the Myanmarese, or Burmese, moved in from the Kingdom of Nanzhao and, by the middle of the eleventh century, had established the Pagan Empire which unified most of what we call Burma or Myanmar today. The Pagan Empire disintegrated in 1287 and several rather smaller kingdoms – including Arakan, Ava and Hanthawady – emerged as the more significant centres of authority. By 1600 the Toungoo Dynasty had brought all of these kingdoms, and the various minor Shan states, under their control and established Burma as one of the most significant nations in South Asia.

In the later eighteenth century the Toungoos were replaced by the Kongbaung Dynasty, which remained the dominant political force in Burma for more than 100 years. A series of wars with Siam (Thailand) and China achieved only marginal gains for either side and, in the early ninth century, King Bodapaya started to look

1   *A few of the 200,000 labourers who helped to construct and maintain roads through incredibly challenging country. (Courtesy of Mrs Angel Benions/A.W. Hickman,* The Dawn Comes Up Like Thunder *(AB/AWH))*

west to expand his kingdom, conquering Assam and Manipur. This brought Burma into greater contact with the British, who waged three major wars between 1824 and 1885, when they finally completed the conquest of Burma. In part, the establishment of British colonial rule was an exercise in protecting northern India from Burmese expansion, but it was also a reaction to the French acquisition of Indo-China (modern-day Vietnam) and a desire to ensure that Britain would be the most significant European power in South and East Asia and serving notice to Siam that the British would not tolerate Siamese territorial ambitions in northern Malaya. Additionally, there was a view that the expansion of British rule and the development of institutions on the British model was, of itself, a desirable objective and, of course, there were bound to be commercial opportunities – not least the prospect of mineral and agricultural development, and the expansion of markets for British goods and services.

Burma changed radically under British rule. A lengthy campaign in the north eventually eliminated local potentates who might become a threat in the future, and Burma was ruled by a colonial administration as, essentially, a province of British India. The advent of the British wrought huge changes in Burmese society and there was considerable economic and social development in the late nineteenth and early twentieth centuries. The opening of the Suez Canal and technological improvements in shipping made it economical to export Burmese rice and teak to Europe, but very few Burmese people benefitted from this. The formation of a British colonial administration attracted large numbers of Indian merchants, who cleared mixed farming communities in order to increase rice production and who engaged in money-lending and land speculation which naturally bred considerable resentment among the local population.

The new government also afforded opportunities in the administration itself and, in the years after the end of the Third Burma War in 1885, the civil service and the courts came to be dominated by the British, Anglo-Indian and Anglo-Burmese, effectively excluding Burmese people from power as well as the economy. The Indian population was further enlarged by the development of a railway system. Most of the labour and the vast majority of the administrative staff who would run the system came from India and established their own communities with very little social interaction or integration with the Burmese people.

By the 1920s a nationalist movement had developed largely, though not exclusively, among the Buddhist Burmese. The movement enjoyed some success and by the 1920s Burma had achieved its own legislating body and a degree of autonomy within the structure of British India, and there were moves afoot to ensure greater Burmese participation in all the arms of government. However, any hopes that these concessions would be enough to bring about a general acceptance of British rule were, at best, optimistic. Unlike India or Malaya, Burma had a long-established tradition of being a single – if not always very united – political entity. Although the developments of the 1920s

CHARLES PAWSEY MC

Sir Charles Ridley Pawsey served as a lieutenant, and later captain, in the Worcestershire Regiment during the First World War, during which time he won a Military Cross for gallantry. At the outbreak of the Second World War he was the District Commissioner for the Naga Hills area and was known as a staunch advocate of the liberties and well-being of the Naga people. He stayed in Kohima throughout the siege and could be seen visiting posts and generally doing whatever he could to bolster morale and support the efforts of the garrison commander, Col Richards.

were reasonably popular, they fell far short of Burmese nationalist aspirations; they did little or nothing to the benefit of the mass of the population and, if anything, helped to further the influence of the Anglo-Indian and Anglo-Burmese communities.

The nationalist movement, though itself divided along political, cultural and regional lines, continued to grow in strength and a spate of riots in 1934–35 led the British to consider a greater degree of Burmese autonomy, thereby giving Burma a more distinct identity within the imperial structure. A series of initiatives brought about a new political structure for Burma. Under the 1937 Government of India Act, Burma's legislature would wield much more authority, but any process of passing power and influence away from the Anglo-Indian and Anglo-Burmese community was going to be very gradual, so once again, although the measures were not unpopular, they were not enough to undermine the nationalist movement.

The very fact that a degree of self-government had been achieved encouraged people to believe that full independence was a practical proposition; if Burma could govern most of her affairs under the British, why should she not govern all of them as a free nation? These developments did not pass unnoticed in

2 Roads in Burma were prone to landslides and this often delayed the delivery of vital supplies. (AB/AWH)

other quarters. Siam had every reason to have doubts about British colonial ambitions in South Asia and Burmese nationalists enjoyed a good deal of financial and other support from that quarter. Such support was not altruistic; Siam had fought several wars with the objective of incorporating eastern provinces of Burma and this might be more easily achieved in the future if Burma was to leave the British sphere of influence.

Further afield, the Japanese Government also took a fairly active interest in Burmese affairs. Fearing economic and diplomatic isolation, and eager to become the prime power in South and East Asia, Japan had good reason to support any movement which might impede British expansion.

At the same time, the fact that Britain had fought three lengthy and expensive wars to secure Burma, and in doing so had bought a considerable degree of protection for her colonial administrations throughout South Asia, meant that she was not going to abandon those gains easily. Burma had been acquired at a great cost, but, perhaps more importantly, abandoning a colonial possession under any circumstances would be bad for the government of the day at home and equally bad for the worldwide perception of Britain as an imperial power; something that had become, if anything, more significant in the wake of the First World War. A withdrawal from Burma would inevitably encourage national sentiment in British India, where there was growing interest in the prospect of a single Indian Union, which would encompass not only the British-held provinces but also the many princely states which, though nominally independent, were dependent on British protection in war.

Beyond the issues of economic activity or international prestige, Burma was also significant in terms of British imperial defence planning as a part of the wider Far East policy. Through the 1930s Britain built a string of airfields to link India and Malaya via Burma, so that if necessary the RAF presence in Malaya and Singapore could be reinforced relatively rapidly by air rather than

3   Burmese landscape. Much of the campaign took place in mountainous terrain with fast-flowing rivers. (AB/AWH)

Brewster Buffalo

At the beginning of the war against Japan, the RAF only had a handful of fighter aircraft based in Burma, and all of those were Brewster Buffaloes. Originally designed as carrier-borne aircraft for the US Navy, the Buffalo was not a success and large numbers were sold to Britain, primarily for training pilots, though a considerable number – well over 100 – found their way to the Far East where they were used in combat. Despite claims that the Buffalo was perfectly adequate as an air-defence fighter against the Oscars and Zeros of the Japanese Army and Navy air forces, the Buffalo was, in comparison, slow, cumbersome, lightly armed and had very little protection for the pilot.

crating up aircraft and sending them by sea or allotting one or more aircraft carriers.

In general, both the political and military hierarchies were rather inclined to reject the possibility of Japanese invasion of Malaya, or at least to assume that, if an invasion was ever mounted, it would come directly by sea to Singapore and be defeated at sea or by planned or existing island defences.

This attitude dominated defence thinking in the Far East for a generation and continued to do so right up to December 1941, despite warnings from various intelligence agencies and analysts, and the advice of Gen. Broad, who served as commander in chief of the Eastern Army in India in 1940. As early as 1936, the man who would eventually have responsibility for stopping the Japanese in Malaya, Lieutenant General (Lt Gen.) Arthur Percival, had made a report to his then superior, Gen. Dobbie, that there was every reason to believe that a Japanese invasion would, in fact, start in northern Malaya and press south to Singapore; a view confirmed by the events of 1941–42. Although there were many factors that contributed to the Japanese victory at Singapore, two of the chief issues were a lack of modern fighter aircraft and a total dearth of tanks. Given the British commitments in 1941 – home defence, fighter cover for bombing missions and, of course, support of the campaigns in the Middle East – it is hardly surprising that the authorities in London did not feel that they could spare Hurricanes and Spitfires for Malaya. Nevertheless, the failure to provide adequate armoured fighting vehicles was a mistake of massive proportions, since it gave such a huge advantage to the Japanese despite the fact that their own tanks were relatively few in number and rather dated in design. When the invasion started, a large proportion of the Commonwealth troops in Malaya had never seen a tank, let alone undergone training in how to deal with an armoured attack.

A similar attitude held sway in relation to Burma. Japan was not really taken seriously as a threat and rather glib assumptions were made about the impossibility of taking large forces – including armour – through the jungles, forests and mountains that

CHI-HA TANK

Although there was very little combat between armoured vehicles at any period of the Burma campaign, armour was significant despite the relatively modest numbers deployed by either side. The Chi-Ha was the better of the two models most widely used by the sole Japanese armoured unit – 14th Tank Regiment. Earlier Chi-Has carried a 37mm gun, which was later replaced with a high-velocity 47mm weapon for better armour penetration. Weighing in at a little over 15 tons, the Chi-Ha had a cruising speed of about 20mph and a range of over 150 miles (240km). In the first year of the campaign, the Chi-Ha performed well against the Stuarts and Valentines of the Commonwealth forces, but was inferior to the Grants in every way. An improved model – the Shinhoto – became available in the latter stages of the war, but was not a match for either the Grant or the Sherman.

separate Burma from Thailand. Indeed, little consideration was given to the very real possibility that Thailand would allow free transit to Japanese forces to mount such an invasion, despite the fact that it was clearly apparent that Japan had a closer diplomatic relationship with Thailand than any of the European powers.

Japan's interest in Burma was not altogether dissimilar from that of Britain. Burma's mineral and agricultural resources were very attractive to a country with a growing population and heavy industrial demands that could not possibly be met by her own resources. There was also the matter of Japan's role as a major Asian power. Although she had been among the victorious Allies in 1918, the Japanese political establishment felt – with some justice – that she had not been well rewarded compared to the other powers. The annexation of Manchuria and its conversion to a puppet state – Manchukuo – not only led to Japan leaving the League of Nations, but damaged her economic relationships across the industrialised world in general, and most importantly with the United States.

Throughout the 1930s Japan had become increasingly concerned about British expansion in South Asia. The massive British naval base at Singapore was certainly part of a plan to ensure safe communication between Britain's Asian colonies, Australia, New Zealand and India, but it was also a declaration of intent, a statement that the British Navy would be a potent power throughout the Pacific and the South China Sea. The Washington Conference agreements after the First World War had imposed limits on all of the great naval powers of the world, but political and public opinion in Japan saw the constraints as unfair and even derogatory, essentially placing Japan in the second tier of naval powers. Her exit from the Washington agreements in 1936 allowed Japan to renew her fleet and to build more of the vessels that would dominate naval warfare in the future – the aircraft carrier. Japan also needed a general industrial expansion to provide export goods and jobs at home, and this could not be achieved without access to raw materials on a grand scale; but the minerals and produce required could not be obtained due to embargoes which had been put in place by the United States and the European powers as a result of Japan's annexation of Manchuria and her war in China.

In the eyes of much of the political and military establishment of Japan, the only means of acquiring the materials that Japan needed for prosperity and security was a physical expansion of its empire. There were two schools of thought as to how that might be best achieved. Most of the generals favoured a northern policy, expanding Japan's borders into China and Manchuria to obtain minerals that were both vital for domestic production and tradable on the world markets. By 1940 that policy had, effectively, been pursued, but, although it had brought some benefits, the cost

4   Kohima Ridge looking south from the air. (Author's collection)

was very high. The war in China had not turned out to be a quick campaign that would force China to accept an unequal peace, but instead had become a major long-term drain on military resources, and there was no end in sight. The alternative policy, which included the annexation of territories in South Asia, had seemed impractical in the early 1930s since all of the potential targets – with the exception of Thailand – were colonies of France, Britain or the Netherlands or, in the case of the Philippines, under the quasi-colonial administration and protection of the United States.

Defeating the Netherlands and seizing the Dutch East Indies would very probably have been a manageable task for the Japanese armed forces, except for the fact that Britain and France would almost certainly go to war to protect the general principle of European colonialism; furthermore, even if America stood back from the ensuing conflict, she was very likely to provide non-military support to prevent Japanese expansion. The start of the war in Europe in 1939 did not change the picture immediately, but the German offensive of May 1940 revealed the weakness of the European powers. Within a matter of weeks the Netherlands and France had been conquered and Britain was isolated in a struggle against Germany and Italy. The new Vichy Government in France was in no position to protect its colonial administration in Indo-China; the Netherlands East Indies would have to run its own affairs without support from the home country; and Britain was too absorbed in her own defence and affairs in north and east Africa to pay much attention to bolstering her position in the Far East, and remained confident that the United States Fleet at Pearl Harbor would provide enough of a disincentive to any ambitious moves on the part of Japan.

Over the course of the next year and more, the situation continued to tip in Japan's favour. The British Armed Forces and the Indian Army became thinly stretched in the campaigns in Africa and in the Atlantic. An isolated triumph at the Battle of the River Plate did little to disguise the fact that Britain's fleets were already over-committed and that India's remarkably small peace-time army was being stripped bare to provide replacements for the desert and to form new units as part of a huge expansion programme. By the latter end of 1941, the only bulwark for British imperial defence in South Asia was the American Pacific Fleet and the forces already assigned to Malaya Command. Japanese intelligence was well aware of the state of Lt Gen. Percival's army in Malaya; most of the units were under strength or only partially trained, or both; there was not a single operational tank in the whole peninsula; the British, Australian and New Zealand air force squadrons were few in number and were mostly equipped with fighters that were a decade behind the times; and the so-called 'fortress' of Singapore was anything but impregnable, regardless of British propaganda claims. If the Pacific Fleet could be taken out of the equation then Malaya and the Dutch East Indies would be vulnerable to a sudden offensive, and Burma could easily follow.

THE ARMIES

Commonwealth Forces

In 1943 Lord Louis Mountbatten was appointed to head the new South East Asia Command (SEAC). His previous experience as Commander of Combined Operations was of questionable value in Asia, but he was an approachable and realistic leader and, although he was prone to dramatic and innovative initiatives that were not always very practical, he was also open to persuasion and was a steadfast supporter of Gen. Slim. Mountbatten's deputy was Gen. 'Vinegar Joe' Stillwell, an appointment that was politically necessary given the extensive American investment in support of China. However, this led to structural command issues since Stillwell was a subordinate to Gen. Giffard in his role as Commander of Northern Combat Area Command (NCAC), but was his superior in his role as Deputy Supreme Commander of SEAC. General Giffard was instrumental in persuading the Chiefs of Staff to organise East and West African infantry and artillery units into divisions, and having them deployed to Burma where they performed admirably. General Giffard was Gen. Slim's immediate superior and the two men enjoyed a constructive professional relationship. Slim did not, initially,

5   A Grant tank loaded onto a raft for a river crossing. (AB/AWH)

choose a military career, but worked as a primary school teacher and as a clerk in a West Midlands metal business. He joined Birmingham University OTC in 1912 and served at Gallipoli and in Mesopotamia during the First World War. In 1919 he transferred to the Indian Army and served as an instructor at the Senior Officers School at Belgaum. By early 1944 he had risen to the command of Fourteenth Army and had been instrumental in improving every aspect of the formation's existence. He did his utmost to make life bearable for the troops and was a firm believer in the equality of every man in the command, regardless of race or creed; an attitude that did not always sit well with some of his contemporaries. Although Gen. Montague Stopford's XXXIII Corps Headquarters would have responsibility for administering the battle, senior operational control passed to Gen. John Grover, who commanded 2nd Division in the relief of Brigadier (Brig.) Warren's 161st (Indian) Brigade at Jotsoma and Kohima, and the subsequent operations to drive the Japanese 31st Division out of India.

*6   General Stopford.
(Author's collection)*

At Kohima itself, Colonel (Col) Hugh Richards was the garrison commander during the siege. His conduct throughout the battle was exemplary, but he was rather undermined by the commanding officer of 4th RWK, Col Laverty.

One of the most remarkable figures in the Kohima battle was Charles Pawsey, the District Commissioner (DC). Pawsey took an active interest in the well-being of the Naga tribes people of the area for more than twenty years and was very popular throughout the region. His bungalow was the scene of intense fighting and the famous 'battle of the tennis court' was fought in its garden. He continued to campaign for fair treatment of the Naga people even after Burmese independence.

The strategic objectives of the Japanese offensive in March–May 1944 was to prevent the Allies from gaining the initiative and mounting a campaign to recover Burma, and to do so by destroying IV Corps of Fourteenth Army around Imphal, before pressing on into northern India. The role of 31st Division was

LEE AND GRANT TANKS

Designed in 1940 and coming into service in 1941, the original Lee tank weighed 30 tons, had a large crew and had poor off-road characteristics. The Grant model was essentially the same, but without the small commander's cupola on the turret. The main gun was mounted in a sponson on the hull of the vehicle, which limited overall effectiveness. The Lee and Grant models were outclassed by German tanks in the desert, but were superior to Japanese vehicles in the Far East. Over 6,000 Lees and Grants were produced and they stayed in service in Asia until 1945, though by then they were being steadily replaced by Shermans.

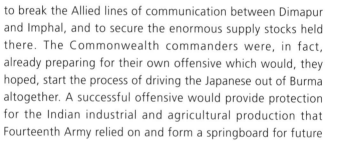

to break the Allied lines of communication between Dimapur and Imphal, and to secure the enormous supply stocks held there. The Commonwealth commanders were, in fact, already preparing for their own offensive which would, they hoped, start the process of driving the Japanese out of Burma altogether. A successful offensive would provide protection for the Indian industrial and agricultural production that Fourteenth Army relied on and form a springboard for future operations to defeat the Japanese throughout South Asia. In turn, that would bring about the liberation of Malaya and Singapore and, in due course, the liberation of the Netherlands East Indies.

In almost every conflict, success is a product of achieving local superiority in manpower and firepower. The nature of the terrain in western Burma and eastern India favoured determined dug-in defences so long as a steady supply of ammunition, food and replacements could be maintained; however, a weak defence could be compromised relatively easily by daring offensive tactics. When advancing, the Japanese tended to attempt to pin the enemy to the front while detaching troops to move around

7 *Medium artillery. (AB/AWH)*

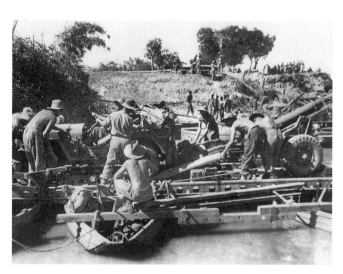

8 *Much of the field artillery had to be towed by jeeps due to the very difficult nature of the terrain. (AB/AWH)*

VICEROY COMMISSIONED OFFICERS (VCO)

The VCO was a distinctive rank in the Indian Army. Senior to Warrant Officers and other NCOs, but junior to King's Commissioned Officers, the VCO was invariably a man of proven abilities. VCOs were to be found in both cavalry (armoured) regiments and infantry battalions. There were three grades of VCOs: in the infantry these were the Jemadar, Subedar and Subedar-Major. Although, in theory, the VCO only had authority over Indian troops, a great many British soldiers were unaware of this and a VCO could generally count on having his orders obeyed. Subedar or Jemadar was a figure of some status and was entitled to be addressed or referred to as 'Jemadar Sahib' by all ranks.

the flanks of the enemy and cut the road behind him, thus cutting off supplies and reinforcements and undermining the morale of the defenders.

When forced on to the defensive, the Japanese relied on strongly built bunkers and trenches, and the determination of the individual soldier to hold a position until told otherwise. Whenever possible, each position would be under observation from others to the flanks and rear so that when a particular strongpoint was eventually captured it would be vulnerable to an immediate counter-attack or could be subjected to intense fire to make it untenable to the Commonwealth troops who had seized it.

The Japanese tactical practice of isolating Commonwealth forces was countered by the development of the 'box' approach, the most famous example being the 'Battle of the Admin Box' at Sinzweya in February 1944, when administrative and line of communication troops supplied by airdrops held out for nearly three weeks. Under this 'box' policy all formations were trained to adopt an all-round defensive posture so that they could hold their position until such time as they were relieved. This was preferable to the formation attempting to break out and re-join the main body of the army; a practice which had led to a tendency to see retreat as the normal option when attacked, resulting in damage to morale and, very frequently, units and formations being forced to abandon stores and equipment to the enemy – so much so that at one point the Japanese were able to field a unit of captured Stuart tanks.

The success of the 'box' approach was demonstrated by an improvement in confidence and morale as it became clear that British, Indian and African troops were more than capable of holding their own against the Japanese, thus reducing the effectiveness of Japanese offensives. It became less practical for Japanese troops to rely on captured stores and the process of fighting for every yard of territory was immensely costly

9   Senior officers in a jeep passing troops at Mandalay. The jeep became a vital tool in the Burma campaign. (AB/AWH)

in casualties. The boxes inevitably slowed Japanese advances to crawling speed, which in turn allowed the Commonwealth forces to locate the enemy more easily and accurately for the deployment of shelling and aerial bombardment.

Naturally, this all had a deleterious effect on the confidence of the Japanese forces and the higher casualty rate forced Japanese formations to transfer men from administrative and support functions to infantry units, thus compromising the general quality of the average soldier on the battlefield. Although the Japanese soldier continued to be a tough and committed adversary, this process of attrition did reduce the efficiency and the élan of the Japanese Army as a whole, which in turn helped to improve the self-belief of Commonwealth troops.

Maintaining a continuous front in either attack or defence was clearly impractical given the nature of the countryside and the immense distances involved, so the few road and river routes and mountain passes became even more significant than would be the case in other theatres. These factors meant

25-POUNDER GUN

The standard field artillery piece of the British Army for twenty years, the 25-pounder was, strictly speaking, a 'gun-howitzer' since it could be fired at both lower register (0–45 degree) and upper register (45–90 degree) elevation; though in the extreme reaches of upper-elevation firing, it might be necessary for the crew to dig a pit to accommodate the recoil of the barrel. Devastatingly accurate to a range of about 14,000yd (12.8km), the 25-pounder was a reliable and popular weapon, and is still in use for training purposes in several countries today. In other theatres, the gun and its thirty-two-round limber were towed by a 'Quad' tractor, although, in Burma, a good many were lightened so that they could be towed by a Jeep.

10   25-pounder guns; a workhorse of the Commonwealth artillery arm. (AB/AWH)

that a great proportion of the fighting was conducted at very close quarters compared to operations in Europe or the desert, and battlefield casualties were very high on both sides. For the Japanese, casualty evacuation was often an almost insuperable difficulty and a great number of soldiers died who would, in other theatres, have received prompt and effective treatment. Overall, the Commonwealth soldier could expect to get medical attention and be removed, if necessary, to a major hospital far from the fighting. However, at Kohima there was really no means of evacuation throughout the siege and many men were wounded for a second or third time in the aid stations.

In keeping with the policy of imperial defence developed after the First World War, the British and Indian armies, along with those of all the other dominions and colonies, shared a broadly common system of organisation. The advantages of a pan-imperial military system are obvious: combining units from different territories and cultures into large formations was comparatively straightforward; arms and ammunition could be produced in several countries (Lee-Enfield rifles are still made in India to this day), and common training programmes made cross-posting of officers from one army to another relatively easily, so long as the men concerned could acquire the relevant languages. There were certain economic implications as well. Since each part of the British Empire was, to a certain extent, responsible for paying for their own defence, adopting the same weapons reduced the unit cost of arms, ammunition and other equipment. Virtually everything was either British-made or produced under licence in the different colonies or dominions.

However, the system was far from perfect. Dominion counties such as Australia and Canada were not necessarily bound by British plans and policies in wartime. Even when there was a shared general strategy British leaders could not simply decide on the deployments of dominion troops, but would have to take account of the foreign and domestic policies of those countries to a far greater extent than would be the case for India or the African colonies. Additionally, although British officers could obviously learn the language (or languages) of their men, it was a time-consuming process and involved finding large numbers of instructors. This was more of an issue with Fourteenth Army than any other formation due to the wide variety of cultures involved – in 1944 there were about forty different languages in use and a wide variety of cultural needs. Indian troops required rice and flour for chapattis, while British ones needed bread and potatoes. Muslim troops could not be given pork and Hindu troops could not be issued with that staple of the British Army, corned beef. It would also seem that no one was ever happy to see the soya link sausages which formed a major part of the diet of frontline troops; they figured regularly in personal accounts of the conflict and were widely, if not universally, loathed.

As if the Commonwealth army did not face enough difficulties in the early stages of the campaign, there were

3.7IN HOWITZER

Often referred to as a 'mountain gun', the 3.7in howitzer came into service in 1917. It is mostly associated with action in North Africa, Italy and Burma, though considerable numbers were used in Europe as well. The gun could fire a 20lb (9kg) shell to a range of nearly 6,000yd (5.5km). It could fire high explosive and smoke shells, and a High Explosive Anti-Tank (HEAT) projectile was designed for use in Burma. A reliable weapon, it could easily be towed by virtually any vehicle available to the Commonwealth forces and could also be broken down for mule transport.

several manpower issues over and above the question of sheer numbers. The rapid expansion of the British and Indian armies had resulted in men who were not physically suited for frontline service being posted to combat units. The formation of large numbers of new battalions required substantial quantities of experienced officers and non-commissioned officers (NCOs) to train the new recruits, thus weakening existing units. These men had to be replaced and many of the newly promoted officers and NCOs who took their place were not really fit for the task. This was even more of a problem for Indian units due to language problems, and a considerable proportion of these officers were not, initially at least, able to communicate adequately in the different languages required. To some extent this was offset by the viceroy commissioned officers (VCOs), which were selected from men with good soldiering and language skills, and who had demonstrated leadership abilities. A VCO was junior to the king's commissioned Indian officers (KCIO), but senior to warrant officers and NCOs. Unlike a KCIO, a VCO only had authority over Indian troops, but it was a position of some status and a VCO would be addressed as 'sahib' by all and sundry.

The trained manpower shortage was exacerbated by the extensive losses in North Africa in 1940–41. Large numbers of experienced officers, VCOs and NCOs assigned to new units in training were drafted back to their original battalions to bring them up to strength, but could not be replaced easily despite an enormous expansion of officer, VCO and NCO training schools and courses. This process was known as 'milking' and inevitably hampered the training schedules – and quality – of the new battalions. The morale and confidence of Indian troops was not helped by the heavy losses in Malaya where many Indian (and British and Australian) troops were sent into battle with virtually no training at all, let alone training for such a challenging environment against a very determined enemy. Additionally, both in Malaya and Burma, unrealistic assumptions were made about the ability of Indian and African troops to adjust to jungle conditions, as very few of either were recruited from jungle areas and had no more familiarity with the environment than troops from England or Scotland.

11   Commonwealth troops manning a light anti-tank gun. Although there was relatively little Japanese armour deployed to Burma, anti-tank weapons proved to be very useful against Japanese bunkers. (AB/AWH)

BREN GUN

Essentially of Czech design, the Bren was exceptionally accurate to about 550yd (500m) and weighed 22lb (10kg). Although the magazine was designed to take thirty of the same .303 bullets as the Lee-Enfield rifle, it was preferable to load only twenty-eight to reduce the risk of jamming. The basic structure of the rifle section was built around two component parts, each carried by a member of a two-man team – one member carrying the Bren gun itself, and the other carrying a spare barrel, spare magazines and a tool kit. The Bren was usually fired from a prone position with a bipod and acted as additional section-level fire support.

None of this was helped by a widely held prejudice against Indian Army troops among the British military hierarchy, despite the exemplary service of Indian divisions – most famously in the East Africa and North Africa campaigns. This was more than a question of race or culture as British officers in the Indian Army were often as much subject to prejudice as their men. This could extend to the very highest ranks. Lieutenant General Lewis Heath was appointed as a subordinate to Gen. Percival in Malaya, despite having a very good command record and being superior in rank, whereas Percival had no senior combat command experience whatsoever. As the war went on, the degree of racial and cultural prejudice did diminish, partly because it became clear that Gen. Slim – an Indian army officer himself – would not tolerate it, and partly through the professionalism and commitment of Indian soldiers at all levels. The first real Commonwealth victory in Burma – the defeat of 55th Division in 1943 – was very much the achievement of 5th Indian Division under Major General (Maj. Gen.) Harold Briggs, of whom Gen. Slim wrote:

12 General Slim. (Author's collection)

General William 'Bill' Slim

Born in 1891, William Slim's family could not afford to send him to university and the first phase of his career was spent as a primary school teacher, and later as a clerk in a metal pipe factory. Although he was not a student, he was able to enlist in the Officer Training Corp of Birmingham University and was able to procure a commission as a second lieutenant in the Warwickshire Regiment at the outbreak of war in 1914.

Slim was wounded at Gallipoli and served in Mesopotamia. He chose to stay in the Army after the war and was admitted to the Indian Army staff college at Quetta in 1926. When war broke out again in 1939 he was posted to command 10th Brigade in the 5th (Indian) Division and took part in the successful East Africa campaign to liberate Ethiopia from the Italians. He was wounded in an airstrike in January 1941 and, in the following May, was promoted to the command of 5th (Indian) Division, which he led in the Anglo-Iraq war and in the invasion of Persia (modern-day Iran).

In March 1942 he took command of Burma Corps (Burcorps), then XV Corps and then of the newly formed Fourteenth Army. The failure of the Commonwealth army in Burma prompted him to reorganise his forces and embark on an intensive training schedule. He dispensed with most of the Army's motor transport in order to reduce dependence on roads and reliance of supplies of petrol, and also to make his troops fit to meet and defeat the Japanese.

The speed and audacity of the Japanese offensive of 1944 took Slim – and his staff – by surprise, but he recovered the situation quickly through tremendous skill and determination, inflicting a defeat from which the Japanese Army in Burma never recovered.

After the war Slim became the first Indian Army officer to be appointed as Chief of the Imperial General Staff (promoted to field marshal), a post he held for nearly four years before moving on to become the Governor General of Australia from 1953–59. Field Marshal Slim died in London on 14 December 1970, aged 79.

I know of few commanders who made as many immediate and critical decisions on each step of the promotion ladder and none who made so few mistakes.

(William Slim, *Defeat into Victory*)

Throughout the British Empire the basic building block of the infantry was the regiment. In peacetime a regiment might have one or two regular battalions, and one or more reserve or territorial battalions. The advent of war in 1939 brought a huge expansion of infantry, armoured and artillery regiments and, therefore, particularly in the infantry, a regiment might have half a dozen or more battalions serving in different divisions and in different theatres. The battalion structure itself varied a little from time to time and from place to place, but was fairly consistent in principle. Typically there would be four rifle companies of about 130 men divided into four platoons of thirty each, comprising three rifle sections of ten men each. In practice it was very rare indeed for a battalion in combat to operate at anything like full strength and it was not uncommon for the battalion to operate as three companies, or for each company to have only three platoons instead of four. Additionally, there would be a headquarters (HQ) company and several specialist platoons and sections; the mortar, carrier, machine-gun and anti-tank platoons, and the pioneer, signals, medical and engineer sections. In total, therefore, the battalion should have had a theoretical strength well in excess of 700, but very often the figure would be as low as 600 and frequently even less if the unit had been in action for any length of time. When the RWK were deployed to Kohima there were only 446 men of all ranks, and this was not an extraordinarily low figure.

The rifle section was the basic building block of the infantry unit and would, nominally at least, consist of ten men, eight armed with the Lee-Enfield .303 rifle, one carrying a Bren gun and the remaining man – often the lance corporal (L/Cpl) or corporal (Cpl) commanding the section – carrying a submachine-gun, either a Sten or a Thompson. The No. 4 Lee-Enfield was the standard model throughout the Burma campaign, though a variant – the No. 5 model, sometimes referred to as the 'Jungle Carbine' – did go into production early in 1944; numbers were limited and the weapon was not popular with the troops due to a poorer balance and doubts about accuracy. The No. 4 model was a remarkable piece of equipment and proved to be reliable and accurate in every theatre of the war, regardless of climate.

The Bren gun, like the Lee-Enfield, was a dependable weapon. Not unduly heavy and easily maintained, it was popular with the troops. One of the riflemen would be designated as the 'No. 2' of the Bren team and would replace magazines as required and periodically change the barrel to prevent overheating. The Sten, on the other hand, was widely hated. Designed and produced as an emergency stop-gap measure in 1940, the Sten was prone to jamming and generally seen as an awkward and sub-standard piece of kit, though German soldiers in the desert and in Europe found that, with a bit of care and the application of a file here and there, it could be a dependable item, so much so that a great many were produced and issued to *Volkssturm* units in 1945 and, apparently, to some armed police forces in German-occupied territories.

Section tactics largely revolved around the Bren gun. In theory, every man in the section carried two magazines for the gun – this requirement defined the shape of the webbing pouches worn at the belt – but this was found to be less than practical. If the section became scattered under fire then it would be difficult to pass the magazines to the gun, so it became normal practice for the No. 2 to carry a box or satchel filled with magazines, in addition to his rifle and the spare barrel. Each man was issued with conventional fragmentation hand grenades, and smoke grenades could be made available but do not seem to have been very widely used.

The other significant platoon-level weapon was the 2in (5cm) mortar. Weighing about 10lb (5kg) and with a barrel length of 21in (53cm), the weapon fired a high explosive or smoke bomb weighing just over 2lb (1kg) to a range of approximately 500yd (450m). The original design included a sighting device, but this was soon abandoned in favour of pointing the weapon toward the target area and relying on the operator's judgement and experience to set the elevation. The platoon would normally carry one 2in mortar and a team of two could manage to discharge eight rounds a minute with reasonable accuracy, but it was a challenge to carry adequate quantities of ammunition.

The battalion's internal support included a platoon equipped with either four or six 3in (7.5cm) mortars. The Mk 1 variant, which was universal at the start of the Second World War and remained in service until at least late 1943, had a range of 1,600yd (1,450m). This proved to be considerably inferior to the German equivalent, prompting the introduction of the Mk 2 model with a range of approximately 2,800yd (2,500m). Both models had a barrel length of 4ft 3in (130cm) and weighed 112lb (50kg). The 3in mortar could be carried over modest distances by the men of the platoon, but only at the cost of having a very limited supply of ammunition. In North Africa and Europe the mortar platoon would generally travel in Bren Carriers, but in the harsh environment of Burma this was often impractical and many units were provided with mules for the purpose, though Jeep transport was not unknown.

By the summer of 1944, the PIAT anti-tank weapon had become available to Commonwealth troops in Burma. Theoretically they were issued on a basis of one to each platoon, though quite often they were not taken into action, particularly in jungle areas where Japanese tanks were very few and far between. The PIAT could, however, be used against bunkers and it was an effective anti-tank weapon. In June 1944, 19-year-old Ganju Lama of 1st Battalion 7th Ghurkha Rifles won a Victoria

Cross in an action at Ningthoukhong in which – though already badly wounded in both hands – he used a PIAT to disable two Japanese tanks in quick succession before engaging the crew of the second one as they dismounted.

The battalion machine-gun platoon would, as a rule, consist of four Vickers guns, but several units managed to 'acquire' an extra gun or two. The Vickers gun itself was not especially heavy at approximately 25lb (11.3kg), but the tripod – depending on the precise model – would weigh at least the same again so, coupled with the substantial quantities of ammunition required, the sections of the machine-gun platoon had a considerable burden to hump up hills, through jungles and across swamps and rivers. On the other hand, the Vickers was exceptionally reliable in the sustained fire role and was a popular weapon – except when being carried. Like the mortar platoon, the machine-gun company would generally have had Bren Carriers for transport, but in Burma these were often replaced with mules. The Vickers and the Bren gun both took the same .303 round as the Lee-Enfield rifle, thus simplifying ammunition supply. Based on the Maxim machine-gun, the Vickers was cooled by a jacket around the barrel, which held nearly 1 gallon (8 pints) of water. As the water boiled around the barrel it turned to steam, which evacuated into a small tank on the ground beside the gun where it would condense and then be fed back into the jacket. The Vickers was fed with canvas belts of 250 rounds and a rate of fire of 450 rounds per minute could be maintained for long periods though it was possible for a competent crew to discharge about 10,000 rounds in an hour with no ill effects to the weapon. The guns would generally be deployed in pairs, but might be brigaded together to provide a machine-gun barrage to cover an advance or suppress the enemy.

Each battalion was, nominally at least, one of three forming a brigade, and each brigade one of three forming a division, though in practice battalions might be switched between brigades and

The British Soldier

Unlike other European countries – or Japan – Britain, and the British Empire and Commonwealth, had a long tradition of maintaining a small professional army. The universal conscription that had been required from 1916 was abandoned very shortly after the end of the First World War.

Until the threat of Germany became too great to be ignored, British governments had reduced defence spending to very low levels and the army in particular had been starved of funds. The Military Training Act of 1939 required all men aged between 20 and 21 to undertake six months' service, but that did little to enlarge the army and full universal conscription was introduced on the outbreak of war in 1939, though there was a wide range of exceptions for reserved occupations, including dock and farm workers, miners and shipbuilders.

In general the standards of both health and education were low, and the problem was exacerbated by the system of enlistment. Many men preferred to serve in the RAF or Royal Navy, which starved the army of recruits, and the men allotted to the army were allocated to units with no regard to their existing skills or experience, or even physical fitness; a substantial proportion of men from poorer backgrounds suffered from the effects of malnutrition in their childhood and had to be 'built up' before they could cope with infantry training. Because of Britain's highly industrialised economy, a greater proportion of conscripts came from factories and other commercial backgrounds, and a far greater number of women took up employment in industry compared to other nations. A typical army conscript might spend six to eight weeks in basic training before being assigned to a unit on a more permanent basis, at which point he would spend some months learning the skills of his new trade in an infantry, armoured or artillery unit. A good deal of such training proved to be of limited value in the field and local commanders were obliged to set up schools to train or re-train men to a standard that would enable them to become effective soldiers.

divisions as circumstances required. Of the thirteen divisions that served in Fourteenth Army, only two – 2nd and 36th – were British, though each of the twenty-four brigades in the eight Indian Army divisions included one British battalion, which was not the case in the three African divisions.

Each division would, in theory, have a reconnaissance regiment of armoured cars or scout cars, carriers and half-tracks. The division's artillery element consisted of three regiments of field artillery equipped with either 25-pounder guns or the 3.7in (9.4cm) mountain howitzer (a high explosive anti-tank round was developed specifically for service in Burma) and an anti-tank regiment with 6-pounder anti-tank guns. The relative scarcity of Japanese armour meant that the anti-tank regiment would frequently be used in the sort of 'infantry gun' role common to other armies of the period and be deployed against pill-boxes and bunkers; consequently, both high explosive and smoke rounds seem to have been more widely used in Burma than elsewhere. Commonwealth forces enjoyed a real advantage over the Japanese in terms of artillery support: the 25-pounder was probably the finest field gun of the period; communications and fire control were better; and a small number of field regiments were equipped with self-propelled guns – an artillery piece mounted on a tank chassis – which naturally provided much better mobility. Additionally, there was not usually a critical shortage of ammunition. This was not the case for the Japanese, particularly at Kohima where ammunition had to be carried along dreadful paths over mountains and through the jungle on pack animals.

By the time of the U-Go offensive, the Commonwealth forces had also achieved a marked advantage in armour. At the start of the Burma conflict in 1942, Commonwealth armour had been limited to a small number of the Rolls-Royce India Pattern Armoured Cars – slow vehicles with very light armour and mounting a single Vickers machine-gun. Once the campaign was under way, 7th Armoured Brigade was diverted to Burma from North Africa. It had originally been intended that the brigade would go to Malaya, but this was pre-empted by the fall of Singapore in February 1942. The brigade took part in the retreat to India and was forced to abandon a considerable number of its Stuart tanks, which were captured and pressed into service by the Japanese.

The armour situation had improved enormously by the end of 1943. The Valentine tanks which had been deployed to Burma from the North Africa campaign – where they had been hopelessly outmatched by the German tanks and anti-tank guns – proved to be utterly unsuitable for the terrain and the climate in Burma, and in any case were not capable of matching the better Japanese models on the battlefield. The American-built Stuart (or 'Honey') tanks that had been committed to the earlier stages of the campaign were mechanically reliable and reasonably fast, but they too had been outclassed and outgunned by the better Japanese models. Even so, they were useful vehicles and continued in service as reconnaissance and infantry support vehicles until the end of the war. The big change was the arrival of the M3 Lee and Grant models which were issued to British and Indian armoured units in 1943. Although these vehicles were obsolete in comparison to German armour and were being replaced by Shermans just as quickly as they could be built and shipped, they were more than a match for the small number of Chi-has and Kyu-Go tanks available to the Japanese Burma Area Army.

In the early stages of each campaign in the war in South and East Asia, the Japanese army and navy air forces had achieved virtually total air superiority in a matter of days. Allied aircraft had been few in number and the majority were obsolete or simply unsuitable for the tasks assigned. By early 1944 this was no longer the case. The RAF and RIAF had procured better aircraft and had developed better combat techniques. Japanese aircraft

THE 'KNEE' MORTAR

The Type 89 Grenade Discharger was widely known to Commonwealth and American troops throughout Asia and the Pacific as the 'knee mortar', from a mistaken belief that it could be fired when bracing it against the thigh. Apart from the fact that this would hardly provide a stable platform for firing, the recoil generated would almost certainly break the operator's leg. Grenade dischargers were issued in very large quantities to offset the relatively low availability of equivalents to the 3in mortar used in Commonwealth units; whole squads might be equipped with these weapons and a battalion might easily have more than fifty distributed through the rifle companies. The discharger was first issued in 1929–30 and remained in service throughout the war, utilising smoke, high explosive and fragmentation projectiles.

design had not really kept pace with Allied aircraft development and Japanese industry and flying schools could not make good the increasing losses suffered in battle. The advantage gained was not, perhaps, so marked as it would have been in other theatres due to the difficulty of identifying targets in the densely forested terrain, the weather conditions that pertained through much of the year and the ability of Japanese columns to move at night with excellent discipline.

Combat air support was also often hampered by the fact that opposing troops frequently engaged at much closer quarters than elsewhere. Even so, airstrikes on line of communication assets, bridges, ferries and railway junctions did have a significant effect on the Japanese logistical effort. The Commonwealth forces also held a major advantage in air transport. The Chindit operations and the various 'box' actions could not have been sustained without effective air supply, though often the constricted nature of battlefields meant that a considerable

13   Gurkhas advancing with tanks to clear the Japanese from the Imphal-Kohima Road in North Eastern British India. (Author's collection)

proportion of airdropped food and ammunition fell to the Japanese. Air transport was, however, limited in quantity and the delivery of material was subject to strategic considerations; thus Slim and Mountbatten were obliged to wrestle with the American authorities to procure or retain transport aircraft on several occasions.

Air transport was a critical factor in what is, arguably, the most famous aspect of the war in Burma – the Chindit operations. Named for the guardian statues that stand before many Burmese temples, the Chindit operations were of questionable value in strategic terms, but they were very good for the morale of the army as a whole and helped to bring some recognition to the forces engaged in Burma since the army was now achieving tactical victories over the enemy. The drawbacks were, however, considerable. The initiative required a lot of manpower and, for the later expeditions, several of the better units in the army were committed to Chindit operations, thus weakening the army as a whole. Slim – and others – were not too happy about the diversion of resources, which he saw as being out of proportion to the results, but he was unable to reduce these heavy commitments since Brig. Orde Wingate, the instigator of the plan, had the ear of the prime minister.

Wingate, a committed fundamentalist Christian, had served in the British Army in the Palestine Mandate in the 1930s, where he had been instrumental in arming and training Jewish defence groups against Arab raiders. His experience had led him to believe that guerrilla tactics were the only viable approach to the Burma campaign, though he failed to understand that an insurgency only prevails once it stops striking from the hills and forms a more conventional administration.

Wingate believed that forming a specialist brigade for extensive operations over several weeks, or even months, behind Japanese lines to sabotage railway and other installations would have strategic benefits. The Japanese would be forced to deploy units in the interior of Burma to protect their lines of communication, which would obviously remove troops from the frontline. In addition, the operations would give a clear signal to the people of Burma that they had not been abandoned by the British and would – if successful – help to restore morale in the army by demonstrating that the Japanese were not invincible. The project enjoyed enthusiastic support from Winston Churchill, who – like most politicians – was attracted to dramatic 'short cut' operations.

Accordingly a brigade group – 77th Brigade – was formed from one British, one Ghurkha and one Burmese battalion. Once in the field, the brigade would operate as seven columns, each over 300 strong and consisting of two reinforced rifle companies, with additional engineering and reconnaissance platoons, and a string of seventy mules to carry the food, ammunition and the explosives that would be needed for the destruction of railway lines, bridges, tunnels and culverts. The brigade received arduous jungle training and men who were not physically fit were posted to other units. The force was to be resupplied by air, but there was no provision for the extraction of men who were wounded or fell sick. Men who could not march would, therefore, be left to die of their injuries, to starve, or to submit to the mercies of the Japanese.

The columns of 77th Brigade spent nearly four months in enemy territory and covered well over 1,000 miles (1,600km) before making their way back through Japanese lines into India. The units suffered heavy losses and by the time they rejoined the army they were utterly exhausted, half starved and racked with illness. In a strategic or tactical sense very little had been achieved other than sabotage of nuisance value, but a great deal had been learned about the war with the Japanese. Despite the high casualties – more than a quarter of the men had died and a very large proportion of the survivors would not be fit for battle again for many months, if ever – the operation was considered an overall success. The experience gained helped to improve training throughout the rest of the army and the operation was positive proof that the Japanese soldier was not invincible. Wingate's Chindit operations had made the Japanese Army aware of the potential threat to their lines of communication by long-range penetration forces and to the impossibility of guarding every bridge and railway installation in the region, but the effectiveness of the operation as a whole was questionable.

The mission had succeeded in diverting Japanese forces from the main front, but at a considerable cost and it was not clear that the absence of the Japanese units which had been diverted had really had as much of a long-term impact on the wider campaign as had been hoped. On the downside, Gen. Kawabe, leading the Japanese forces in Burma, came to the conclusion that moving large bodies of troops through Burma and into India was not as difficult a challenge as he had previously thought, and this was a factor in persuading him that a major offensive to the west in early 1944 was a viable proposition.

The apparent – or claimed – success of the first Chindit penetration encouraged Wingate to pursue a similar project, albeit on a much larger scale, and he was successful in getting Churchill's support for an operation that would consist of no less than six brigades. He even proposed that the whole army should adopt a guerrilla policy and might have been successful had it not been explained to Churchill that this would allow the Japanese to ignore the columns and march rapidly to seize the airfields on which the columns would have to depend when they were in the field. Wingate now developed a new approach. Instead of marching through Japanese lines and into their rear, the units would be airlifted and delivered by parachute and glider to various points, where they would build strongly fortified bases from which mobile columns would emerge and disrupt Japanese communications.

Superficially this might seem to conform to the guerrilla tradition of establishing strongholds in favourable territory, but in fact merely gave the Japanese targets that were easily identified and could be contained. By chance the Chindit forces were committed in areas that were crucial to the Japanese plans for early 1944 – Operation U-Go – and had a major effect on the wider campaign since large quantities of men, artillery and very scarce imperial airpower had to be allocated to reducing the Chindit forces. Whether the British, Indian and African units involved – highly trained and confident in themselves and one another – would have been better employed in the main battle is open to debate, but – as in 1943 – Chindit losses were heavy. Wingate himself never saw the end result of his labour; he was killed in an air crash on 24 March 1944 and was replaced by Brig. Walter Lentaigne.

The Imperial Japanese Army

Lieutenant General Masakazu Kawabe was appointed to the command of the Japanese Burma Area Army in March 1943 after having seen extensive service in China. He was persuaded – against the better judgement of his staff and various subordinate commanders – to promote an ambitious strike against the Commonwealth forces at Imphal and Dimapur, and then into India. The plan – Operation U-Go – was the brainchild of Lt Gen. Renya Mutaguchi. Lieutenant General Mutaguchi had led the 18th Division during the campaign in Malaya in 1941–42 and was confident that the Commonwealth forces in Burma would collapse in the face of a rapid, determined offensive. While the bulk of his force marched on Imphal in March 1944, one division – 31st Division under Gen. Sato – was dispatched to take Kohima en route to the Allied railhead and depots at Dimapur.

The plan struck Sato as being completely unrealistic; he had no confidence in the ability of the Burma Area Army to provide the necessary logistical support and was highly doubtful about Mutaguchi's low opinion of the Commonwealth forces facing him.

Contrary to common belief, there was not a great deal of jungle training – if any at all – for Japanese soldiers prior to the invasions of Malaya and Burma. Although some units did undergo training and took part in exercises on Hainan Island from March 1941 onward, the majority had to depend on their basic infantry training. Rapid success in Malaya and Burma gave the Japanese soldier an aura of competence, but his overall ability in the jungle was not particularly notable – he was just as likely to get lost, injured or suffer from disease and infection as any other soldier. Significantly, however, he was encouraged not to be afraid of the jungle, and his training and culture encouraged a far greater degree of self-reliance than the soldiers of other armies. Japanese troops were conditioned to expect very little in the way of supplies; the priority was always ammunition, with rice rations supplemented by rather irregular issues of tinned or dried food. Sheer survival in the battle area was dependent on active and effective foraging, even when the war was going well, and became an enormous challenge in the later stages of the campaign as many thousands of Japanese soldiers simply starved to death.

Resourceful and determined, the Japanese soldier led a hard life. His pay was pitifully low and throughout his service he was subject to a high level of brutality. Severe beatings from instructors for the most minor infringements or failures were a normal part of the training process, to the extent that it was not uncommon for a man to be permanently crippled or even killed. There was even a practice of 'self punishment'; two men who had committed an offense, even at the most trivial level, could be set to beat one another until ordered to desist.

The strict military code was combined with a rigid system of rank and racial status. Korean and Taiwanese soldiers were seen as being racially inferior to the Japanese and received even worse treatment. The victory in Malaya and initial success in the Dutch East Indies, Burma and the Philippines encouraged a belief that the Europeans were inferior even to the Koreans and Taiwanese,

14   Japanese anti-tank rifle. Virtually ineffective against the later models of Commonwealth tanks, the anti-tank rifle was still a potent weapon against Bren Carriers and armoured cars. (Author's collection)

15   Japanese flag. (Author collection)

which further bolstered confidence in racial superiority and – perhaps more importantly – the Japanese soldier was imbued with a belief in his emperor as an infallible and divine person descended directly from the gods.

In reality, emperors had been subject to a succession of regents for many generations and had little control over any aspect of policy. This goes some way towards explaining the decision of the Allies to allow Hirohito to continue as emperor after the end of the war, though really it was much more a matter of retaining a superficial appearance of preserving the existing political structure against communist influence. Hirohito escaped blame for the war and responsibility for atrocities in China, Malaya, Singapore,

JAPANESE PISTOLS

The Japanese Army adopted only one revolver, the Model 26. It was a double-action, 9mm six-shot weapon based largely on Smith and Wesson designs of the late nineteenth century. The most common automatic pistol was the Type 14 Nambu, which fired a low-velocity 8mm round. Neither model was especially popular and, since Japanese officers were obliged to provide their own side arms, many of them chose to purchase foreign models privately or to acquire them on the battlefield. The Nambu was quite accurate, but was prone to jamming. Something in the region of 200,000 Nambus were produced between 1906 and the end of the war in 1945.

Indonesia, the Philippines, Indo-China, Burma and throughout the southern Pacific, though, in theory at least, he could have prevented the progress to war by demanding the resignation of civilian ministers or generals.

The manpower demands of the war were too great to be met by the Japanese population and for this reason – and for political and propaganda purposes – efforts were made to recruit from other sources. Before the Malaya campaign had come to an end, Japanese officers were already busily trying to raise units from captured Indian soldiers. Initially this met with little success, despite a very understandable feeling among the troops that they had been, at best let down and at worst betrayed. Many Indian soldiers had been posted to Malaya with very little training and then put straight into combat with no opportunity to adjust to the climate. British command had been totally incompetent, both tactically and strategically, and many of the British officers were scarcely better trained than the men themselves and often had an inadequate grasp of the appropriate language. Given the absence of air cover, no armoured support and poor communications which hampered

General Kotoku Sato

Born in Yamagata Prefecture in 1893, Kotoku Sato joined the Army after high school and graduated from the Army Academy in 1913. As commander of 75th Infantry Regiment (a Japanese regiment equates roughly to a British Brigade Group, with three battalions and various integral supporting arms) he mounted a successful operation against the Russians at the Battle of Lake Khasan in 1938. In March 1943 he took command of the 31st Division in China and, after a short spell in Thailand, he took his division to Burma in September of that year.

General William Slim considered Gen. Sato to be:

> … the most unenterprising of all the Japanese generals I encountered. He had been ordered to take Kohima and dig in. His bullet head was filled with one idea only – to take Kohima. It never struck him that he could inflict terrible damage on us without taking Kohima at all. Leaving a small force to contain it, and moving by tracks to the east of Warren's brigade at Nichugard, he could, by 5 April, have struck the railway with the bulk of his division. But he had no vision, so, as his troops came up, he flung them into attack after attack on the little town of Kohima.
>
> Slim, William, *Defeat into Victory*

He was deeply unhappy about the prospects of the 1944 offensive and, when it failed, refused to take his own life, demanding a court martial which he believed would clear his name. For fear that such a court martial would reflect badly on his superior – Lt Gen. Renya Mutaguchi – it was arranged that Gen. Sato would be declared to have had a breakdown and would be unfit to stand trial. Sato returned to duty in 1945 with no official stain on his record. He spent the post-war years looking after his former comrades and was instrumental in building a number of war memorials. General Sato died in 1959.

Arisaka Rifle

Although the Arisaka had been designated as the standard rifle of the Japanese Imperial Army and Navy, a good many of the previous rifle used – the Type 38 – remained in service, since it had proven impossible for Japanese industry to produce Arisakas in the volume required. Generally dependable, the Arisaka took five 7.7mm rounds in a short box magazine – half the magazine capacity of the Lee-Enfield carried by Commonwealth troops. It was not as accurate as the Lee-Enfield at longer ranges, though in practice an infantryman seldom saw a target more than 300yd (275m) distant. Large numbers of Arisakas were issued to Chinese troops after the war, and by Indonesian insurgents against Netherlands forces. The bayonet for the Arisaka was a well-designed weapon, complete with a curved quillion which could be used to hook around an opponent's weapon, at which point a deft twist could disarm him.

the use of the artillery, they had every reason to feel aggrieved and it is remarkable that so few men volunteered for service in the Japanese-sponsored Indian National Army (INA) in 1942. The following year, however, saw a marked increase in recruitment. The British seemed to be failing to make any progress – the more so since the Japanese had control of the media – and conditions in the POW camps were deteriorating. For many it must have seemed that their only hope of avoiding starvation and returning to India was to join the fight on the Japanese side. In total the INA would eventually grow to a strength of about 40,000 by the end of the war, roughly half of whom were former Indian Army soldiers, but was never regarded, either by the Japanese or the Commonwealth commanders, as a first-class formation.

The Japanese Soldier

The typical 'Heitai' or Japanese infantryman or gunner – like most servicemen the world over – was not a professional soldier, but a civilian drafted for military service. About one third of all Japanese conscripts came from a farming background and another third from factories and commerce, which would have a major impact on industrial and agricultural production as the war progressed. The heavy losses increased demand for conscripts, particularly for the infantry.

The majority of the men enlisted were well educated compared to their counterparts elsewhere; virtually all of them had completed an extensive elementary education and about 10 per cent – possibly more – had some familiarity with English.

New recruits were required to be at least 5ft (1.5m) tall and weigh 110lb (50kg). Conscription had been part of Japanese life since 1873 and the peacetime enlistment was for two years, which in theory was extended to three years in time of war, though very few men were released to return to civilian life.

A very large proportion had had some degree of military training before they went into the service. Once they were inducted, they underwent very rigorous training in conditions that can only be described as brutal. Beatings were a normal part of military life and were meted out for even the most minor infractions. Recruits might be ordered to inflict 'self-punishment' whereby two men would have to beat one another. Basic training lasted for about four months, which was followed by another four months of unit and field-craft exercises.

Officers were expected to develop a closer relationship with their men than was the case in most countries, sharing the same food and conditions. Japanese troops were very poorly paid – officers were expected to purchase their own uniform, sword and even their own pistol.

16 A typical Japanese soldier. (Author's collection)

The other significant Japanese formation was the Burma Independence Army (BIA), though much of its membership consisted of groups of bandits who adopted the BIA as a justification for their activities. The Japanese were under no illusions about this and, although the BIA did perform some useful service, they were not generally issued with arms or equipment and were expected to arm themselves from captured or abandoned Commonwealth supplies. In August 1943 the Japanese declared Burma to be an independent country and installed a puppet government under Ba Maw. The BIA was now reformed as the Burma National Army and eventually grew to seven infantry battalions which were, from that point, rather better supplied by the Japanese. However, they continued to be treated as racial inferiors, with every Burmese soldier, including officers, obliged to salute even the lowliest private soldier in the Imperial Army, including the Koreans.

The Japanese Army saw very little in the way of development of arms through the war years in comparison with the United States, Britain or Germany. In part this was simply a matter of demand: so long as there was no great incidence of armoured warfare there seemed little value in investing in a major development and replacement programme for the armoured units. In fact, Japan never really developed an armoured doctrine as such: only one armoured unit – 14th Tank Regiment – served in Burma and they were so short of equipment – even in 1942 – that a whole company of the regiment was equipped with captured Stuart tanks.

The Japanese system of military organisation differed somewhat from that of the Commonwealth and had more similarity to the German and American models. The permanent unit of administration in the infantry was the regiment. The size and structure of the battalion varied in different theatres, so it is only really possible to give a rough idea of the numbers and equipment that might be involved.

17   Riflemen with the Arisaka rifle. (Author's collection)

The regiment consisted of three infantry battalions and various regimental assets, including a gun company, and was thus roughly comparable to a British or Indian brigade; however, the battalions themselves were larger and, at full theoretical strength, typically comprised about thirty officers – a rather smaller group than in a Commonwealth battalion – and over 1,000 men; roughly 25 per cent more than the British or Indian equivalent. Broadly speaking, the battalion would include the HQ and a gun platoon with two Type 92 howitzers. The Type 92 was a light 70mm piece with a range of about 3,000yd (2,745m); it could fire ten rounds per minute with a well-trained crew and utilise three types of shell – high explosive, armour piercing and smoke. Additionally, the battalion would have an ammunition platoon to support a machine-gun company of three platoons with four guns each and, in some cases, a mortar platoon equipped with two 90mm mortars. Both the mortars and the battalion guns could be broken down for transport by mules or ponies. Animal transport was extremely significant in Burma and a full division might have as few as 150 motor vehicles – and even these might be dispensed with due to the terrain – but might have well over 2,000 mules.

The four rifle companies would, at full strength, have a company HQ and three platoons consisting of three rifle squads and a grenade discharger squad, each thirteen men strong. The rifle squads were issued with adequate small arms which stood up to the Burmese climate fairly well, and the shortage of mortars at battalion level was offset by the large number of grenade dischargers. These weapons were roughly equivalent to the 2in mortar of the Commonwealth forces and were often referred to as 'knee mortars' from a mistaken belief that they could be braced against the leg for firing – a practice which would very likely have broken the leg of the operator.

Japanese anti-tank weapons were an area of serious weakness. A wide variety of anti-tank weapons were developed, including a reasonably effective dedicated 47mm anti-tank gun and armour-piercing rounds for most existing weapons, but Japan did not develop a real equivalent to the PIAT or Bazooka and an innovative anti-tank rifle grenade failed to live up to expectations. Anti-tank rifles were considered adequate at the beginning of the war when Japanese soldiers seldom encountered anything heavier than a Bren Gun Carrier or an obsolete armoured car, but were not very effective against Valentine or Stuarts tanks and were virtually worthless against the Lee and Grant tanks deployed from 1943 onward. A number of effective expedients were developed based on satchel and pole charges, but these could only be used at great risk to the operator.

Much of the artillery was horse-drawn, but horses did not fare well in Burma and were very difficult to replace. This was not as

18 *A speeding Ha-Go Type 95 tank. (Author's collection)*

anachronistic as it might seem, though, as the horse was still an important asset in warfare. Germany and the Soviet Union were still heavily dependent on the horse even in 1944 and both countries had cavalry formations right up to the end of the war. An artillery regiment would be attached to each division and might typically consist of three battalions, one with three companies of six 75mm field guns and two armed with medium howitzers, although the distribution of weapons varied considerably throughout the war years. The weapons themselves were often of a decent standard, though there were serious shortages of shells and the production quality of ammunition was suspect. The artillery arm was further hindered by poor radio communications between infantry and artillery units, and by a lack of adequate maps which greatly reduced the effectiveness of indirect fire.

The Armies

The units that fought in Burma, Malaya and the Pacific in 1942 were determined and courageous to an incredible degree, but their ranks were dramatically reduced by disease and battle through 1942 and 1943, so a great many replacements were required. These men were generally not so fit and well trained and many of the men serving in infantry units in 1944 would not have been acceptable for infantry service in 1942. However, they did have the benefit of the experience of the veterans in their battalions and overall standards remained high, so long as the campaign was going well and adequate supplies were provided. Although the army was in good spirits overall, there was a serious lack of confidence among the senior commanders when the U-Go offensive was being planned. Several highly experienced and skilled officers had grave doubts about the ability of the supporting arms to maintain the levels of food and ammunition required and several felt that insufficient regard was being given to the abilities of the enemy.

Although the Allied Arakan offensive of 1943 had not been a success, bringing it to a halt had been a much harder business than might have been expected on the basis of the 1941/42 campaigns in Malaya and Burma. The Commonwealth troops on the ground were much more capable than they had been in the past and there was no prospect of gaining air superiority. Equally, although the objectives of Operation U-Go were overly ambitious, failure to launch a major offensive would simply allow the Commonwealth forces to grow in strength and confidence. Adopting a defensive policy would simply have handed the initiative to the enemy at a time when Japanese forces across the Pacific were already in retreat and Japan herself was increasingly subject to American air raids, which were demoralising the population and decimating industrial production. General Mutaguchi's plans may not have been welcome, but the alternative was surely a long, slow and costly retreat through Burma against an enemy who was only going to grow stronger.

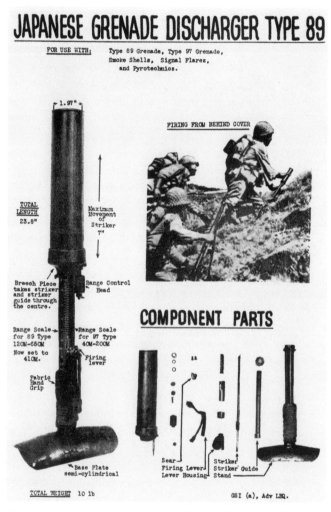

19   *The Japanese knee mortar grenade launcher. (Author's collection)*

THE DAYS
BEFORE BATTLE

It is very difficult to appreciate the sheer scale of Burma, as the Mercator projection generally used for globes and atlases is very misleading since it effectively enlarges landmasses in the north while shrinking those nearer the equator. Extending to the better part of 250,000 square miles (647,000 sq km) Burma is much the same size as France and Belgium combined, and with its huge mountain ranges and thick forests and jungles it is a desperately hard country to fight in, even without consideration of the weather. The western aspect of Burma consists of three ranges of mountains – the Arakan Yomas in the south, the Chin Hills in the centre and to the north, and the Naga Hills. In practice these effectively form one gigantic chain of mountains stretching over 600 miles (965km) from the small coastal town of Gwa in the south until they meet the Brahmaputra valley in the north. The highest of these ranges – the Naga Hills – rise to 12,000ft (3,650m), but even in the lowest range – the Arakan Yomas – peaks in excess of 5,000ft (1,500m) are not unusual. In addition to the precipitous nature of the mountains, they are covered with thick forest and jungle to about 6,000ft (1,830m). There are very few passes and, until 1941, there were no all-weather roads that penetrated from west to east, only a modest number of difficult

MULES

A hybrid between a horse and a donkey, the mule has a rather undeserved reputation for being stubborn. Easier to maintain than horses and much more powerful than a donkey, mules were used extensively in Burma by both sides. Generally weighing between 750–1,000lb (340–450kg), a mule can be expected to carry about 150lb (70kg) and march for 20 miles (32km) without resting.

tracks, most of which were extremely challenging at the best of times and virtually impassable during the long rainy season which generally begins in May and comes to an end in October.

For a century or more before the Japanese invasion of 1942 there had been a number of plans to build roads through the mountains which would connect the central plain of Burma with the road and rail systems of Assam in north-west India, but none had come to fruition largely because importing and exporting goods by sea was relatively quick and cheap. The eastern aspect of the central plain is bounded by the Karen and Kachin hills, which run from north to south. The challenging terrain is further complicated by three great rivers which flow southward from the Himalayas – the Chindwin, the Irrawaddy and the Salween. Each of these runs into the Gulf of Martaban to the north of the Andaman Islands and each of them constitutes a major barrier to east-west communication. Only the lower reaches of the Salween are navigable, but the Irrawaddy provides a communications route for nearly 1,000 miles (1,600km) from the sea to Myitkyina and the Chindwin can carry river traffic nearly as far north as Kohima, which lies high in the Naga Hills more than 50 miles (80km) to the west of the river.

Despite the geographical challenges of the country, Burma was an attractive proposition for commercial development. Until the

20   A convoy approaching Kohima. (AB/AWH)

21   A convoy on the Kohima Road. (AB/AWH)

22   A landslide blocking the road – a common event in Burma. (AB/AWH)

twentieth century, the chief exports had been rice from the central plain and teak from the forests, but in 1942 there were two other significant factors – oil from the Yenangyaung fields and wolframite from Mawchi. The value of the former is self-evident, but the latter was of particular importance in wartime. Wolfram was the major source of tungsten-based materials (which is why 'W' is the periodic table abbreviation for tungsten) for electric light-bulb filaments and – crucially in 1942 – the basis for armour-piercing ammunition. Other important minerals included nickel, silver and tin, which was in short supply since the Japanese occupation of Malaya.

These resources were significant to both sides. Shortages of rice would be a destabilising influence in both Japan and India, and although Japan could obtain wolfram from other sources, Burma provided more than one third of the wolfram available to the British Commonwealth. Equally, although both sides could acquire oil from elsewhere, there was a value to denying it to the enemy and either side could make savings on transport if more accessible supply could be secured.

In addition to these economic issues there were major strategic considerations. As long as Japan was embroiled in a war of conquest in China, her resources would be heavily stretched elsewhere, but in order to keep China in the fight she would need to have a steady stream of ammunition, arms, vehicles and fuel from American and Commonwealth resources which could only be delivered via Burma. A huge amount of this material was produced by the industrial complex of northern India and, so long as Burma was denied to the Japanese, the factories and railway systems would be safe from air raids. Moreover, Burma also provided the means of communication between India and Britain's colonial possessions in the Far East, which were – until the campaign of 1941–42 – the chief source of rubber and tin for the Commonwealth war industries. Burma was also the only practical route for transferring aircraft to the front in the event of a Japanese invasion of Malaya.

23 Crossing the Irrawaddy River. (AB/AWH)

Finally there were political imperatives, for the British administration of Burma had to face a variety of challenges. In addition to the simple matter of the natural resentment of a foreign power – though given Burma's social and cultural divisions this was not a universal factor – economic development had encouraged a good deal of immigration from India. This was not limited to technical, administrative, commercial and managerial workers, but had included a large number of money lenders and land speculators who were – rightly or wrongly – widely seen as exploiting Burma and denying opportunities to the local population.

The focus of organised political resistance to British rule was the Thakin party, which largely depended on students and Leftist political activists. The outbreak of war in Europe in 1939 encouraged the Thakin party to become more assertive in their campaign for independence. Naturally, this presented an opportunity to Japan and several Thakin leaders made visits to Tokyo in search of political and material assistance for their cause.

Naturally enough, the pro-independence movement was further encouraged by the rapid defeat of Britain and the Netherlands in Malaya, Singapore, Hong Kong and the Netherlands East Indies in 1941–42.

Removing Burma from external control by the Government of India did little to assuage the appetite for independence, but it certainly complicated the military situation. Under new arrangements for partial autonomy, the administration of Burma became responsible for her own defence, albeit under the oversight of British Imperial military structures. Following the general pattern of British military arrangements in India and the Far East, the armed forces available for the defence of Burma consisted of a small number of regular British army units and larger numbers of locally enlisted units with a high proportion of British officers and NCOs. Although Burmese autonomy had made political sense in 1937, the military rationale was far less practical. Toward the end of 1940 Burma had become part of the operational responsibility of Far East Command with its HQ in Singapore.

Since Burma was obviously crucial to the defence of India, the Commander-in-Chief, Gen. Wavell, travelled to London in September 1941 and attempted to have operational control transferred back to India in the belief that this would simplify administrative and operational issues. Although French Indo-China (Vietnam) was, by this time, under effective Japanese control, Wavell's request was turned down despite the support of the Governor of Burma, Sir Reginald Dorman-Smith. Wavell renewed his request in November and gained the support of the Chiefs of Staff in London, but the Defence Committee decided to put off implementing any decision until the new Commander-in-Chief Far East, Sir Henry Pownall, had time to take up his appointment and it was not until three days after the Japanese landings at Kota Bahru, in north-east Malaya, that the decision to transfer Burma's operational control to the HQ in India was finally enacted.

In 1937, when Burma was granted autonomy and became responsible for her own defence establishment, it was generally accepted that there was no great risk to her borders from neighbouring countries: India was secure in British control; Thailand was considered far too weak militarily to mount an invasion and was, in case, vulnerable to a British counter-stroke though Malaya; Indo-China was held by the French who had little, if any, interest in expanding their Asian colony; and China to the north was already heavily engaged defending herself against a Japanese invasion. Outside of the major towns and cities there was relatively little hostility to British rule – certainly not enough to indicate an imminent armed insurrection and war of independence. Broadly, Burmese security was seen as more a matter of policing than military action. This being the case, the military establishment was very modest for such a huge country.

When Burma became a separate entity from India there were nine battalions of the Burma Military police which were converted, in name at least, to infantry battalions and were renamed as the Burma Frontier Force. In addition there was a complement of two British infantry battalions – though these units had been stripped of officers and specialists for roles in Britain and India, and had been reduced to roughly half of their theoretical establishment – and four battalions of the Burma Rifles with a small element of engineers and a single battery of mountain artillery. The war in Europe prompted a degree of expansion, including a volunteer formation – the Burma Auxiliary Force – which was recruited from the Anglo-Burmese, Anglo-Indian and European elements of the community and which was largely committed to the defence of the oil installations. Due to the demands of other theatres of war, there was very little to spare for Burma in the way of arms, equipment, money or manpower.

The problems of the Burma command were exacerbated by the expansion itself. Trained officers and NCOs were transferred to new units to assist in training the recruits, with the inevitable

LEE-ENFIELD RIFLE

The Lee-Enfield rifle design was already fifty years old by the outbreak of the Second World War. Although there had been a number of minor adjustments over the years, the basic weapon of most soldiers in every section of every platoon was virtually the same as the one which had been carried by his predecessors in the Great War. Mechanically robust and reliable, and tremendously accurate, the Lee-Enfield had a calibre of .303in and a ten-round box magazine and continued its service as the primary rifle of the British Army until 1956.

consequence that the existing units were seriously weakened twice over. The existing units lost experienced soldiers and a considerable proportion of the men promoted to take their place were not really up to the task.

Equipment was, if anything, even more of a challenge. A single anti-aircraft regiment was raised in 1941, but it received no guns until after the opening of the Japanese campaign in Malaya and consequently had had very little practical training before the opening of hostilities in Burma. Beyond that there was a dearth of even the most basic items, such as rifles, machine-guns, mortars, transport, grenades and small arms ammunition were insufficient for training purposes, let alone for combat.

The situation in the air was even worse. At the start of the campaign the RAF had one squadron of sixteen fighters equipped with the obsolete Brewster Buffalo, and there was one squadron of the American Volunteer Group (the famous 'Flying Tigers') whose Curtiss P.40 Tomahawks were certainly a great improvement over the Buffalo, but were less manoeuvrable than the Japanese Zero and Oscar fighters.

Despite the clear warnings that war with Japan was, if not absolutely imminent, certainly a distinct possibility in the near future, very little was achieved in the way of putting civil administration on a war footing. Some effort had been made to form an Air Raid Precautions (ARP) establishment, but shortages of suitable materials and labour coupled with difficult geological conditions in most urban areas resulted in there being very few effective air raid shelters, and there was no facility for coordinating rail and water transport to meet military needs.

Wavell was well aware of the problems and did everything he could to improve the situation, but his plans were thwarted by the opening of the Japanese campaign in Malaya. Troops and material – including armour, a divisional headquarters and aircraft – were diverted to Singapore and a series of misunderstandings damaged relations with the Chinese Government, which had committed large numbers of troops to northern Burma despite the fact that they were urgently needed at home.

All of these chickens came home to roost when the Japanese invasion commenced. Although the various infantry battalions

24 Loading a pack howitzer onto a raft for a river crossing. (ABI/AWH)

had been grouped together into brigades, there had been no opportunity to train the Brigade HQ, or to accustom the individual battalions to operating as teams within brigades or higher formations. There were virtually no anti-tank weapons and a complete dearth of training to deal with armoured vehicles. Japanese air raids caused panic among the civil populace and a great throng of refugees tried to make their way to India, which not only blocked the roads but stripped the dockyards of the skilled labour required to unload the military stores being delivered to Rangoon.

Reinforcements of aircraft achieved some early success against the Japanese Army Air Force which persuaded the commander of Fifteenth Army to abandon the bombing of urban centres and to focus instead on the destruction of Commonwealth air power and the support of troops on the ground, though due to poor surface-air coordination this was of limited value. As had been the case in Malaya, Japanese air forces tended to focus on targets of opportunity along the Allied lines of communication.

Outnumbered and outgunned, and despite a number of local successes, the Allied forces were simply not capable of stopping the Japanese advancing through Burma and threatening north-east India. The damage to the Allied cause was extensive. China was now almost cut off from Allied aid and would, for the foreseeable future, have to fight Japan largely on her own slender military and industrial resources. The Allies were deprived of the agricultural and mineral production of Burma, which would now be exploited by the Japanese, though the effectiveness of the Allied policy of destroying well-head equipment, storage tanks and pipelines meant it would be some time before the Japanese could derive any benefit from the Yenangyaung fields, which they captured on 19 April.

At about this time, the Commonwealth forces on the Burma front were organised into a single formation – Burcorps. This consisted of 17th Indian Division, 7th Armoured Brigade, which had been transferred from the desert only a few months earlier, and 1st Burma Division. The latter was more a formation in name than in practice and lacked most of the headquarters and other divisional assets required to perform its duties adequately. Command of the corps was given to Gen. William Slim, who arrived from India to take charge on 19 March. Slim would go on to have a profound effect on the whole Burma campaign, but there was little he could do to check the Japanese advance without a massive injection of infantry, artillery and, above all, armour so the longest retreat in British Military history continued until mid-May, when the rearguard of Burcorps passed into Assam and brought the campaign to a close.

The effect on the morale of the British, Indian and Burmese troops was as significant as the loss of equipment – much of which had been abandoned during the retreat. British prestige in Asia, already undermined by the defeats in Malaya, Singapore and Hong Kong, fell even further, while the reputation of the Japanese

25   Commonwealth troops in action in the Arakan. (AB/AWH)

armed forces was considerably enhanced. The liberation of Burma was clearly going to be a long, drawn-out affair and would require the total rebuilding of the British and Indian forces at a time when there was already an excessive demand on the war industries.

The Japanese invasion drew to a halt at the Chindwin River for several reasons: the coming of the monsoon would hamper any further advance and then rains would reduce the viability of the tracks that would carry their supplies. Additionally, although their combat formations had enjoyed great success, it had come at a price. Battlefield casualties were not insignificant and there had been heavy losses to disease, so the units needed time to reorganise, re-equip and assimilate replacements.

For the Allies, a massive invasion to drive the Japanese out of Burma completely was out of the question; Wavell had already started planning for an offensive in the Arakan, but the administrative and operational command structures were obviously inadequate. A series of operations was considered for late 1942, but only one was really pursued – an advance by 14th Indian Division (commanded by Maj. Gen. Lloyd), which had been formed in June of the previous year. 14th Division was among the first formations to be equipped with the conditions of Burma in mind. In place of the normal quota of heavy trucks, the division had ten transport companies, four equipped with jeeps and six with mules. As a new formation it naturally had no experience and a good deal of the training received was of limited value. To complicate matters further as the operations progressed, additional brigades were committed to the fight until, eventually, 14th Division HQ had nine brigades under command, which represented an impossible burden. By the end of January 1943 it had become abundantly clear that nothing was being achieved and the operation was eventually halted on 5 February. The Japanese response was to mount a counter-attack and, throughout May, 55th Division drove Commonwealth forces northwards.

26   American supply trucks on the Burma Road. (AB/AWH)

On 14 April Gen. Slim was given command of all the Commonwealth forces in the Arakan. His first objective – since he really had no choice – was to concentrate his force in an area out of contact with the enemy where it could rebuild and train for a new campaign. Although it was generally accepted that no major

GENERAL WILLIAM 'BILL' SLIM

A popular and skilled leader, Slim was eager to promote good health facilities and educational opportunities for the troops. Army schools, teaching everything from basic literacy to civics, sprang up all over northern India. In part, this was to give soldiers something to do other than drink and get into trouble, and in part this was to give them better options when they returned to civilian life. In order to give the troops some sense of liberty when they were on leave, Slim tried to set up 'no-saluting' zones in leave areas, but was prevented from doing so – Army authorities feared it would undermine the authority of the officers.

Slim encouraged innovation to offset equipment shortages by using materials that were available locally, such as the introduction of 'parajutes' – parachutes made from jute – for dropping supplies, and a temporary road surface made from bitumen and hessian.

offensive could be undertaken until November 1943 when the monsoon season passed, there was also a need to carry the war to the enemy in some way. It would be very bad for the morale of the army to have achieved nothing in a year of campaigning and it would give the Japanese every opportunity to rebuild their own formations, consolidate their gains and establish their administration throughout Burma. A major conventional offensive was clearly out of the question, but the first of two long-range penetration operations was launched, though with questionable results.

Late in the year, a major reorganisation of the Eastern Army took place, leading to the creation of Fourteenth Army under Gen. Slim. The new army consisted of IV Corps, based out of Imphal under Gen. Scoones, and XV Corps under Gen. Christison in the Arakan. Given the widespread prejudice against Indian Army officers, Slim's appointment was remarkable, though he was very obviously the right man for the job, and he set about transforming the Commonwealth forces in Burma into a well-trained and efficient force. Slim was also ultimately responsible to another new figure, Lord Mountbatten.

Mountbatten had been appointed as the head of another new organisation – South East Asia Command (SEAC). Mountbatten and Slim were both eager to carry the fight to the enemy, and both realised that the campaign could not be won by the Chindit operations – though they accepted that the Chindits could make a valid contribution to the progress of the wider strategy. Equally, both were all too well aware of the fact that the British and American political leaders – Churchill and Roosevelt – had agreed to pursue a European policy: that the Allies would focus primarily on the defeat of Nazi Germany before turning their attention to Japan. Inevitably this meant that resources were hard to come by for Fourteenth Army and, consequently, Mountbatten's objectives for 1944 were not as ambitious as he would have liked. Three Chindit brigades were sent across the Chindwin to converge around the Meza Valley to disrupt Japanese lines of communication and prevent them deploying reinforcements to the north. In this area, Stillwell's Chinese forces were making progress; Scoones' IV Corps mounted operations toward the Chindwin; elements of Christison's XV Corps advanced on either side of the Mayu Mountains and toward Maungdaw; and 81st (West African) Division moved down the Kaladan Valley.

Each of these offensives encountered the Japanese in rather greater strength than had been expected, which confirmed the conclusions of Commonwealth intelligence staffs. The participation of the INA (generally described as the 'Japanese Indian Force' or 'JIFFs' in commonwealth circles) was seen – by Gen. Mutaguchi at least – as a significant factor in the enterprise. He had revealed his plans to Subhas Chandra Bose, the political leader of the INA. Bose had, in turn, discussed the venture with

Bhagat Ram Talwar who, in addition to being a leading communist in the Indian independence movement, was also a double agent working for British intelligence. Although he had been forewarned, Slim was limited in his options. Plans were already detailed for IV Corps to mount an offensive eastward into Burma and, by chance, this was to occur at much the same time as the Japanese would be moving west toward Imphal, Kohima and then – if successful – deep into India.

The railway to Dimapur was already operating at full capacity and could not be expected to maintain substantial reinforcements; also, the divisions of IV Corps had been prepared for offensive operations and were not, therefore, ideally placed to react to a Japanese attack. This was, in fact, part of the rationale behind Mutaguchi's conviction that a major offensive was the only practical course of action. He believed that the Commonwealth forces were still weak in combat compared to his own troops, but that if they were allowed to continue to build up their strength, expertise and confidence they would mount their own invasion of Burma. He was equally sure that any such offensive would grind to a halt in the face of Japanese resistance, but also believed that if the Commonwealth forces made any progress at all – and they were almost bound to make some – it would prove very difficult to dislodge them.

The Allied Arakan offensive of the previous year had been a costly failure, due partly to poor training and low morale among the troops, and partly due to failures in administration and supply. Even so, Mutaguchi was aware that the Commonwealth troops were starting to come to terms with jungle warfare and would become an increasingly formidable enemy in the future. Additionally, he knew that his own situation was not going to improve any time soon. The Japanese Army was heavily engaged in China and across the Pacific, so he could not hope for much in the way of replacements, let alone reinforcements, and there was no prospect of improved equipment, particularly armour.

General Mutaguchi's 1944 U-Go offensive was ambitious and daring, and if successful would have been a remarkable accomplishment, but it was extremely optimistic. His force was considerably weaker than Slim's Fourteenth Army, though the ratio of combat troops to line of communication units was rather higher. It was a very dangerous gamble for several reasons. Mutaguchi's logistical arrangements were poor, so in addition to the relative numerical weakness of the artillery arm, shortages of ammunition were virtually inevitable, particularly for Sato's 31st Division which would have to rely on mule trains traversing incredibly difficult terrain. Additionally, the invasion force would not be able to count on the air superiority that they had enjoyed in 1942 and the armoured element, though not particularly significant for the force advancing on Kohima, would be at a severe disadvantage in terms of both numbers and quality.

Despite opposition from his own staff and his subordinate commanders, Mutaguchi was successful in persuading his superiors, Gen. Kawabe, Field Marshal (FM) Terauchi and Prime Minister Hideki Tojo, to authorise the operation. Orders were given on 19 January for an attack on Imphal, accompanied by a diversionary attack into the Arakan (Ha-Go offensive), and the intention was that the entire operation would be complete before the start of the expected monsoon rains in May.

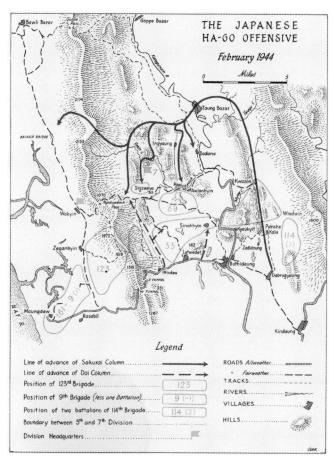

Map 2   The Japanese Ha-Go Offensive, February 1944. A diversionary operation designed to force Slim to commit forces in the Arakan, well away from the targets of the main offensive against Imphal. (Butler, p.140)

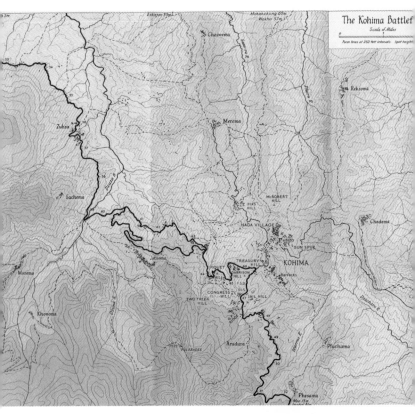

Map 3   The Kohima area. (Butler, p.360)

THE BATTLEFIELD

Opening Manoeuvres

On his own initiative, Gen. Renya Mutaguchi, commander of the Japanese Fifteenth Army, expanded the scope of Operation U-Go far beyond the original objectives, which had been agreed with his superiors to encompass a major attack far deeper into India. Mutaguchi's staff and immediate subordinates – the commanders of 15th, 31st and 33rd Divisions – were strongly opposed to the expansion of the operation for several reasons. In their opinion the available Japanese forces were not sufficiently strong to take on the Commonwealth forces, the terrain was too difficult and the logistical arrangements too fragile to have much hope of victory. They were aware that the campaigns of 1943 had been successful, albeit at a heavy cost, and that the general quality of the combat units had declined markedly since the invasions of Burma, Malaya, the Netherlands East Indies (Indonesia) and the Philippines in 1942. They were also aware that the Commonwealth forces opposing them had increased markedly in number and that their training, confidence and equipment had improved considerably since the beginning of the conflict.

27 A captured Japanese artillery piece. (AB/AWH)

A major barrier to bringing the operation to a successful conclusion was the logistical challenge. The problems posed by the terrain were enormous and, in many cases, the advancing formations would have to rely on animal transport for supplies of food and ammunition and there would be very limited capacity for evacuating the wounded. General Mutaguchi brushed these objections aside, believing that the fighting spirit of Japanese troops would be enough to sweep the Commonwealth forces before them and capture ample supplies from the vast Commonwealth stockpiles of stores at Dimapur. In his view, the defeat of the enemy would allow a relatively easy passage into India. Despite the misgivings of his subordinates and his own staff officers, however, the operation was eventually accepted by the supreme headquarters in Japan and authorised by Prime Minister Gen. Hideki Tojo.

The major thrust of the campaign would be carried out by 15th and 33rd Division, whose troops would start to move westwards in March. At the same time, 31st Division under Lt Gen. Kotoku Sato would move through the hills and jungles to seize the town of Kohima and then advance to take Dimapur, thus cutting off the only surface resupply route to Imphal. If successful, the Allied forces in Burma would be starved of materiel and reinforcements, but even if the operation failed to reach its objectives in good time, the Allied command would be obliged to deploy forces away from the main battle at Imphal.

General Sato was far from happy about the plan: he saw it as being hopelessly optimistic and based on an unrealistic assessment of the terrain, the capacities of a single division and of the ability and strength of Allied forces. In Sato's opinion, the days when Japanese troops could be confident of always defeating British and Indian troops in battle at little cost were long past. The jungle warfare schools that had been set up under Gen. Slim's command had given Indian and British troops a far greater degree of confidence, and the Chindit operations, though very costly, had demonstrated that Japanese soldiers were not invincible. Sato also had no confidence in his commander, Gen. Mutaguchi, believing him to be petty, unrealistic and unintelligent. He also felt that he had good reason to suspect Mutaguchi's motives in assigning the Kohima operation to 31st Division.

The two men had been members of rival political movements in the 1930s and Sato was sure that Mutaguchi was sending him on a hopeless venture. If the mission was unsuccessful it would not simply be a matter of defeat and retirement, as would be the case in most armies: if Sato failed to achieve his objectives there would be an expectation that he would be shamed and feel obliged to take his own life. Sato could hardly refuse to undertake the operation once it had been sanctioned by Tokyo, but he was sufficiently confident that the initiative would be a failure and warned his own staff that they would very likely not return from the campaign. Sato was particularly concerned about the supply situation and went so far as to warn his staff that they might all die of hunger if they encountered stiff resistance.

En Route to Kohima

1944		
	15 March	31st Division under General Sato crosses the Chindwin River
	19 March	Leading units of 31st Division go into action against 50th Indian Parachute Brigade at Sheldon's Corner
	21 March	50th Brigade concentrates at Sangshak to deny the Japanese a direct approach to Kohima
	26 March	Supply shortages and heavy casualties force Brigadier Hope-Thompson to withdraw from Sangshak
	27 March	31st Division continues its march to Kohima
	29 March	Japanese units cut the Dimapur-Kohima Road
	3 April	4th Battalion RWK arrive at Kohima but are promptly ordered to move to Dimapur
	4 April	Leading elements of 31st Division start to engage at Kohima

On 15 March 31st Division crossed the Chindwin and started the march north-west, making good time despite the difficult terrain until elements of Col Fukunaga's 58th Regiment (a force of nearly 4,000 men) encountered Brig. Hope-Thompson's 50th Indian Parachute Brigade at Sangshak. After six days of heavy fighting, in which his brigade suffered the loss of about 600 men, Hope-Thompson was obliged to withdraw due to a combination of water and ammunition shortages as well as the heavy casualties. Hope-Thompson's defence at Sangshak effectively delayed 58th Regiment's advance to Kohima by a week, and

had seriously weakened their offensive power. Hope-Thompson, therefore, made a major contribution to the successful defence of Kohima, but in a shameful example of professional jealousy he was widely discredited by a raft of rumours claiming that he had had a nervous breakdown. In reality he had conducted the action with skill and determination, and had successfully extricated his brigade despite being surrounded by a much more powerful force.

In addition to the damage inflicted on 58th Regiment, Hope-Thompson's 50th Brigade had captured maps and documents which clearly showed that the Japanese intended to commit an entire division to the capture of Kohima and Dimapur, as opposed to the single regiment that Slim and his staff had estimated as the maximum force that they could assign to the operation.

Kohima lies on the Manipur Road between Dimapur and Imphal, the closest thing to a reliable all-weather route between the two and, therefore, a crucial route for troops and supplies. A single-track road until improved in 1943, it was still a very challenging drive – it might easily take ten hours or more for a truck to traverse the 40-odd miles (65km) between the two towns.

The ridge-top town of Kohima occupies a very strong position dominating the road from Dimapur to Imphal, the crucial communications link from the railhead to the town and plain of Imphal, where Slim intended to fight a major battle that would effectively cripple, if not destroy, the Japanese Army before he invaded Burma. With an adequate garrison it would be a hard objective to carry, but it is overlooked from virtually any direction by the surrounding mountains. The colonial town is situated on a sharp ridgeline overlooking an extensive Naga village. Almost all of the locations were named for military or colonial installations, such as FSD Ridge for the Field Supply Depot, DIS Ridge for the Daily Issue Store, GPT Ridge for the General Purpose Transport depot and Jail Hill for the local prison which lay below it.

HA-GO TANK

The Japanese 14th Tank Regiment fielded three models of vehicle in the Burma campaign: the Chi-Ha, the Ha-Go and, for a while, a company of Stuarts captured from the Commonwealth forces in 1942. The Ha-Go entered service in 1935 and was considered one of the best tanks in the world at the time. It was relatively light and fast, and was armed with a 37mm gun and two 7.7mm machine-guns. The Ha-Go was deployed in large numbers in China and a few hundred were taken into service by the opposing forces of Chiang Kai-shek and Mao Zedong at the end of the war. Production of Ha-Go's came to an end in 1943, but they continued to be a significant part of the Japanese armoured forces until 1945, used largely for reconnaissance purposes.

The road passes along the eastern edge of the ridge and then around the northern point before running west through passes to Imphal. Possession of the town would deny the use of the road to an enemy, but a garrison would be very vulnerable to artillery fire directed from higher ground. The close nature of the countryside – steep hills and a mixture of thick scrub and jungle – means that an attacking force can make a close approach to positions on the ridge with little chance of detection.

Kohima has two other major disadvantages as a defensive location. The ground is very rocky and it is, therefore, extremely difficult to build adequate fighting trenches or dug-outs for command posts, stores and medical facilities. Also, there is very little water. Several water tanks had been constructed on the ridge, but none of them were properly protected against small arms fire, let alone shelling, and there was only a small spring which could not possibly provide a sufficient supply of fresh water for a substantial body of troops.

28   *A dug-out at Kohima. (AB/AWH)*

Kohima 1944

In April 1944 there was hardly a garrison at all, and certainly not one designed to withstand a major assault. There were around 2,500 men in the town at the beginning of the month, nearly half of which were non-combatants and convalescing casualties. The combat troops comprised elements of the Assam regiment which had already seen fierce fighting at Jessami, where they had inflicted heavy casualties on Col Torikai's 138th Regiment; two companies of the Burma Regiment (about 250 men) of the Assam Rifles; a battalion of the Shere regiment of the Royal Nepalese Army which was as yet only partially trained; a modest number of men from 1/3rd Ghurkhas and the Burma Rifles; and elements of an Indian Army Battalion, the 4/7th Rajputs, who joined the garrison early in the battle. With the exception of the Shere regiment, none of these units were present in any strength and, in total, there was only a force of about 1,500 men available to defend the town against Sato's 31st Division, many of who were insufficiently trained and some of who were 'scratch' bodies of men under unfamiliar officers and NCOs. The sum total of artillery in the garrison amounted to one 24-pounder gun which had been allotted for training purposes; however, since the town was used as a major staging post for supplies to Imphal there was a very large stock of food and small arms ammunition.

The arrival of the RWK was obviously a major benefit, but led to a significant command problem. The commander of the RWK, Col Laverty, refused to recognise the authority of the station commander, Col Richards. Laverty went so far as to describe himself as the 'commander of the fighting troops' in Kohima, though in fact he was only the commander of one element of the force and was not responsible for the elements of the various other units present. He frequently undermined the station commander, even refusing to allow him to make use of the RWK's radio equipment to communicate with army command.

The experience of the RWK at Kohima started badly and got worse. After fierce fighting in the Arakan they had been abruptly

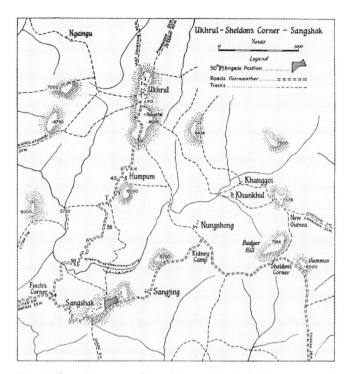

Map 4   The actions proceeding Kohima at Ukhrul, Sheldon's Corner and Sangshak. (Butler, p.248)

pulled out and transported by air to Assam, and by 29 March had arrived with their animal and motor transport at Dimapur. The following day they made their way to Kohima, where they would be joined by the rest of their parent formation, 161st Brigade. On arrival at Kohima the battalion was bombarded with rumours that a divisional-scale attack by the Japanese was imminent, despite courageous delaying actions by the Assam Rifles and the Assam Regiment some 30 miles (48km) to the east of the town, and of 50th Indian Parachute Brigade at Sheldon's Corner and the village of Sangshak. So the RWK set about preparing defensive positions, which was a challenging undertaking given

HURRICANE/HURRIBOMBER

The Hurricane fighter remained in service in the Burma theatre as a frontline combat aircraft until the end of the war, nearly two years after it had been superseded on other fronts. Although it was inferior in several respects to Japanese aircraft, such as the Mitsubishi Zero, the Allies had achieved almost complete air superiority by early 1944 and the fighter-bomber variant – the Hurribomber – was widely used as a ground-support aircraft and flown by several British and Indian squadrons.

the nature of the ground, and before they had time to complete their trenches and foxholes the battalion was moved again, this time back to Dimapur.

The reason for this move and counter-move had been a decision by Gen. Rankin, who was the commander of what was known as 202 Administrative Area. Rankin had received instructions from Slim that his primary task was to ensure that the railhead at Dimapur, along with the huge stockpiles of food, ammunition and other supplies, as well as very large numbers of non-combatant troops and Indian labourers, did not fall into the hands of the Japanese. Rankin's position was unenviable. In an earlier conversation with Slim he had remarked that his ration strength was something in the order of 45,000 men, but that it was unlikely that as many as 500 of them were capable of using a rifle. There were persistent rumours that Japanese troops were closing in on Dimapur (which later proved to be untrue) and Rankin interpreted his orders to mean that Dimapur must take priority over all other considerations. Superficially this was a reasonable assumption since there was little point in having possession of a relative backwater like Kohima if the stores at Dimapur were lost to the enemy; although equally the value of the stores would be very limited if there was no means of transporting them to Imphal.

Initially the situation at Kohima was not viewed with great alarm by Gen. Slim or his subordinates. Clearly Dimapur was the more important asset, but there was also a strong belief that a Japanese attack on Kohima could not be mounted in overwhelming strength. Slim and his staff had calculated that the Japanese would only be able to bring one regiment (three battalions) with very limited artillery assets to bear due to the extreme nature of the terrain they would have to pass through. Therefore, they believed, the Japanese would not commit themselves to a full-blooded assault on Kohima, but would instead leave a modest force there to compromise the existing garrison, while the bulk of 31st Division pressed onto Dimapur, a much more significant location in terms of the 'big picture'. This view continued to hold sway for some days after the general thrust of the Japanese offensive had become apparent.

Although the garrison at Kohima was very slender, General Sato's 31st Division had suffered considerable casualties at Jessami, Sangshak and Kharasom, and the fighting must obviously have been a drain on the relatively slight stock of ammunition that the division could carry. This was not an unreasonable conclusion since Sato himself already had concerns about his supply situation, particularly in regard to ammunition for his artillery. However, the division was still a potent force and, despite the hard trek to Kohima, was in fairly good spirits, enhanced by the prospect of a quick victory. Sato himself was confident of capturing Kohima, pressing on to Dimapur and resupplying the formation at the expense of the Commonwealth forces.

The leading elements of Col Fukunaga's 58th Regiment arrived at Kohima on the evening of 3 April. Of all the three infantry regiments of 31st Division, 58th Regiment had had the shortest and least challenging route, although it had been held up for nearly a week by the action at Sangshak and had sustained a substantial number of casualties. The first battalion of the regiment mounted an attack the following morning as the second and third battalions closed up on the town. The initial Japanese attacks were tentative and dealt with relatively easily by the defending garrison, but clearly they was evidence that a major force had arrived in the area rather earlier than had been expected. As soon as the news of the attacks reached Gen. Stopford's XXXIII Corps HQ, 161st Brigade were ordered to return to Kohima with all possible speed since it was now clear that the Japanese had selected Kohima as a major objective rather than a mere road block which could be contained and by-passed. Of the three battalions of 161st Brigade, only the RWK was able to make its way into the Kohima perimeter during the morning of 5 April before the road was cut behind them, leaving the remainder of 161st Brigade 2 miles (3.2km) to the west at Jotsoma.

This represented a major addition to the infantry strength of the garrison as a whole, but still only amounted to around 450 men, well short of the complement of a full-strength infantry battalion. The majority of the brigade was in contact with the enemy and, therefore, had problems of their own, but they were able to provide some artillery support which would prove crucial to the defence of Kohima. The garrison was now confined to the ridges, spurs and glens that stretched from IGH (Indian General Hospital) Ridge to DIS (Daily Issue Stores) Hill.

The Noose Tightens

1944		
	5 April	RWK return to Kohima in response to Japanese attacks
	6 April	31st Division mount the first concerted attack on Kohima
	8 April	Japanese 138 Regiment cuts the route between Jotsoma and Kohima

During the course of 5 April the Japanese mounted successive probing attacks at Jail Hill to the south of the perimeter and successfully dislodged elements of the Shere regiment overlooking the Naga village to the north. The perimeter held was remarkably small, little more than 1,000yd (915m) from north to south and only about 900yd (825m) at its widest point.

By 6 April the Japanese had finally cut all communication between 161st Brigade and the Kohima garrison and the close siege now began in earnest. A series of attacks by Fukunaga's 58th Regiment succeeded in forcing elements of the Ghurkhas and the Burma Rifles from their position on Jail Hill, driving them onto DIS Hill where they were met by a company of the RWK under Maj. Shaw. The Japanese now occupied positions overlooking the southern aspect of the Commonwealth position, but the cost had been heavy, including the loss of the commander of the 2nd Battalion of 58th Regiment. A plan was made to mount an immediate counter-attack with another company of the RWK, but the Japanese had dug in with remarkable speed and were obviously present in considerable strength, so the plan was abandoned to conserve the fighting strength of the battalion.

Despite the encircling Japanese forces, it proved possible to infiltrate a company of the 4/7th Rajputs before the Japanese cut the telephone line that day. Throughout the night the Japanese mounted repeated attacks from Jail Hill to DIS Hill. The attacks were direct and aggressive with no attempt to outflank or suppress the defenders, which rather suggests that the Japanese commanders believed that the garrison had been shaken by the events of the day to such an extent that they would be prone to panic or despair and could be swept away by a determined driving charge. A counter-attack on DIS Hill revealed that Japanese troops had ensconced themselves among the buildings there and had to be winkled out with some difficulty, but did produce two prisoners, one of whom was able

VICKERS GUN

The Vickers gun was adopted by the British Army in 1912 and became the standard machine-gun for all the Commonwealth countries. It was gas-operated and the barrel was cooled by a water-filled jacket. Despite the tropical heat, the Vickers gun performed admirably in Malaya and Singapore. The gun fired the same .303 calibre bullets as the Lee-Enfield rifle and the Bren gun, but from 250-round canvas belts. Each battalion had a machine-gun platoon, usually with four weapons and with six to eight men per gun; two to operate the weapon and the others to carry ammunition and provide protection for the gun team.

to provide some intelligence relating to Japanese strength and positions in the vicinity.

During the night of 7/8 April the Japanese launched several attacks on DIS Hill and elsewhere at the southern end of the perimeter, and by dawn on the 8th they had recovered their position among the DIS buildings, while at the northern end they were able to push the defenders back toward the Deputy Commissioners bungalow. During the course of the day they had also isolated 161st Brigade at Jotsoma and had managed to bring at least one of 31st Divisions' 75mm howitzers into action.

Although he had succeeded in bringing his force through terrible terrain and concentrating it at Kohima, Gen. Sato had problems of his own. His superior, Gen. Mutaguchi, quite rightly saw Dimapur as being the more important objective and ordered Sato to advance accordingly. Sato was focussed on the immediate problem of Kohima, but could hardly ignore a direct order, so he now sent one battalion of 138th Regiment toward Dimapur. Within a matter of hours Mutaguchi's order was countermanded by the theatre commander, Gen. Kawabe, who was already having doubts about the practicality of Mutaguchi's plans to advance deep into India. Accordingly, the battalion made its way back to the Kohima battle and the threat to Dimapur was lifted. Strategically, however, this was a disastrous move. Although there were a great many troops in the Dimapur area, there were very few combat soldiers and many of these were unfit for battle. It is quite possible that a defence of the stores and railway marshalling yards there could have mounted, but if it had failed the loss of munitions would have been a massive blow to the Commonwealth forces throughout the whole theatre.

The plight of the Kohima garrison was painfully clear to Brig. Warren's 161st Brigade at Jotsoma. Warren's mountain guns were firing on Japanese positions around the town and breaking up attacks on a daily basis, but the prospects of

29 *Defoliation from shelling at Kohima. (AB/AWH)*

JOHN HARMAN VC

Lance Corporal John Harman of the 4th Royal West Kents was the son of millionaire Martin Coles Harman, owner of Lundy Island. Corporal Harman was awarded the Victoria Cross posthumously for his repeated conspicuous gallantry on 8 and 9 April 1944 during the Battle of Kohima.

penetrating the Japanese forces to relieve the garrison were not good. On 9 April Warren mounted an attack on Piquet Hill by 1st Punjab Regiment, which floundered against strong opposition. Things were not going well for the Japanese either: three attacks by 58th Regiment that same night failed to make much impression on the defenders, though there were heavy losses on both sides.

Surrounded

Casualties mounted steadily, which was a two-fold problem for the garrison. Every man killed was a drain on resources and there was the additional complication that the perimeter was so small that there was no safe place for the treatment of casualties. Two things happened on 10 April to make the situation even more challenging. The monsoon rains arrived a month earlier than usual, which to some degree eased the water shortage since men could collect rainwater in whatever receptacles they could find, but on the same day Col Laverty came to the conclusion that his casualties were so heavy that he would have to reduce his commitments by giving up DIS Hill to the enemy and concentrating the remains of two of his companies (C and D) into a single body on FSD Hill.

Clearly the Japanese policy of direct attacks was having an impact since casualties were mounting and the perimeter was shrinking, but the battle was not going to plan and a new approach was adopted. Instead of mounting simple charges against the Commonwealth positions, the Japanese now combined such attacks with infiltration tactics, creeping between the Allied rifle pits to take up sniping positions or to attack individual trenches and foxholes by stealth. Although several counter-attacks were mounted to clear out the infiltrators, there simply were not enough Commonwealth troops available to achieve this. The entire garrison area was already vulnerable to artillery, machine-gun and sniper fire from the surrounding hills and it now became a huge risk to move anywhere within the perimeter without risking life and limb to Japanese infantrymen hiding in the ruins of buildings and abandoned foxholes.

The danger of moving from one location to another was marginally reduced by decreased visibility due to heavy rain, but was exacerbated by the increasing absence of natural cover. Continuous artillery and mortar fire was steadily denuding the ridges and glens around Kohima of foliage. During the night of 11 April three more direct attacks were mounted, followed by an attempt at infiltration. None of these attacks made much progress, but the continual action was steadily wearing the garrison down. Casualties were not especially high, but physical and emotional exhaustion was a more significant issue. The perimeter now enclosed a very small area and no place could be considered safe from snipers, machine-gun and artillery fire by day, or from infiltrators by night.

Another major problem was the loss of two of the doctors and a large amount of medical stores on 13 April when artillery fire struck the Advanced Dressing Station (ADS), killing or wounding men receiving treatment for previous wounds. The following night there was a bit of good news for the garrison: a patrol from 4/7th Rajputs was able to pass through the Japanese lines from 161st Brigade in Jotsoma, a reminder that friendly troops were not that far away. This must have been

30   Extensive air supply operations occurred throughout Burma. (AB/AWH)

balanced, in the minds of some at least, by the question of why, if there was a Commonwealth force only 2 miles (3.2km) away, Kohima had not been relieved over the preceding week? The answer was that the two battalions of 161st Brigade at Jotsoma were not sufficient to mount a major attack that could force a path through the Japanese encirclement and that, if the brigade did manage to force its way into Kohima, it would be at the expense of abandoning the road to Dimapur and thereby granting the Japanese free passage to the great railhead and concentration of stores. Additionally, Warren's brigade could give supporting fire that was absolutely crucial to the survival of the garrison, disrupting or even destroying Japanese attacks on a daily basis. There was no space in the garrison's perimeter where Warren's guns could have been safely deployed – they would have done no more than provide an easy target for Sato's artillery. Equally, there was no space in the garrison to provide positions for two infantry battalions and Brigade HQ. The perimeter was already too tightly packed for that, so it would have had to be enlarged, which could only be achieved by mounting attacks to recover positions already lost and which the Japanese had strongly fortified, the cost would have been prohibitive and there was no guarantee that any such attempts would have been successful.

All things considered, the morale of the garrison continued to be good despite the lack of sleep, water and the difficulties of achieving even the slightest movement, but in a sense there was little choice but to fight on. The near-certain outcome of surrendering to the Japanese was widely understood by all ranks. Moreover, there was a degree of understanding that the Japanese were not supermen, and that they could not continue to bear the level of casualties they were incurring day after day, particularly with their precarious supply situation. To some degree this was offset by the regular acquisition of stores dropped by the RAF, although the surrounding mountain and the unpredictable breezes and current made it very difficult to make accurate drops and, as the perimeter shrank under enemy pressure, it became increasingly difficult to deliver stocks of ammunition and food to the garrison. Consequently, a large proportion of materiel fell into the hands of the Japanese. These 'Churchill supplies', as the Japanese called them, included food, medical supplies and quantities of small arms ammunition, but, more significantly, they contained large amounts of bombs which allowed the enemy to use the 3in mortars which they had captured in the opening actions before Kohima.

FSD Hill and Kuki Piquet

1944	17 April	Kohima perimeter sharply reduced by the fall of FSD Hill and Kuki Piquet to Japanese attacks

| 1944 | 18 April | Punjab Regiment with armoured support makes contact with the Kohima garrison |
| | 20 April | Japanese encirclement broken by 2nd Division under Major General Grover |

Throughout the night of 17/18 April the Japanese at last made some serious progress. They successfully stormed FSD Hill and Kuki Piquet, effectively reducing the garrison's perimeter to an area of less than 400yd (365m) in each direction. If the perimeter had been cramped before, it had now become desperately crowded with combatants, non-combatants and wounded men, as well as being thickly spread with dead Commonwealth and Japanese soldiers and the general detritus of battle.

On the morning of 18 April, however, the first encouraging signs of relief appeared when elements of 1/1 Battalion the Punjab Regiment, with armoured support, at last made contact with the garrison. The men of the Kohima garrison could now be withdrawn from their positions, but the battle was far from over. Desperate attempts on the part of the enemy to finally over-run the remaining perimeter before a full relief could be effected failed to make any headway, but the Japanese were still in position on and around Kohima Ridge and, as long as they remained there, the road to Imphal would be vulnerable.

In the early stages of the battle, 2nd Division had been assigned to the protection of Dimapur. As a whole, the division had no experience of fighting the Japanese. Although elements of 6th Brigade had seen action in the Arakan in 1943, a large proportion of the brigade had been replaced since then. All of the 2nd Division had, however, been trained for combat in Burma. In early April 161st Brigade made its way into Kohima as a relief for the garrison, while two battalions of 5th Brigade – the Cameron Highlanders and the Worcesters – got ready to close the Kohima to Dimapur road. By 17 April a series of

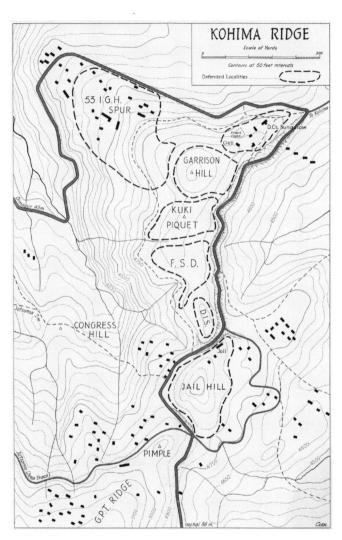

Map 5   Kohima Ridge. (Butler, p.347)

hard-fought encounters had restored contact with the balance of 161st Brigade at Jotsoma. Once the Kohima garrison had been replaced, Gen. Grover, commander of 2nd Division, was faced with the problem of destroying Japanese forces which were, by this time, well entrenched in the surrounding hills. His plan was to ensure that the Japanese were engaged at every point of the battlefield and would, therefore, be unable to reinforce positions by moving troops across their front from one location to another. The general Japanese approach to defence in close country was not to attempt to hold a continuous line, which was effectively impossible in the jungle anyway, but to maintain a large number of well-protected positions and mount aggressive patrolling operations between them to discourage enemy penetration.

This had proven to be an effective approach in the past. Although the individual posts could become isolated and fall to the enemy, so long as the occupants were determined to sell their lives dearly, each post would have to be pounded furiously and then stormed in a close attack, which inevitably caused heavy casualties. In the main these posts were very small, containing only a section or platoon of men, but could absorb the attention of a whole company of enemy infantry for days on end. Fighting of this nature had a damaging effect on the morale of the Commonwealth troops charged with destroying such positions. Hard fighting with heavy casualties, only to find that the objective had only housed a handful of Japanese soldiers in the first place was bad enough, but the realisation that exactly the same sort of objective had to be faced on the next slope, and the next, sapped the spirits of the soldiers. As if that and the gruelling conditions of jungle warfare were not hard enough to bear, the aggressive patrolling of the Japanese between their defended localities meant that the troops could never be at ease since a Japanese patrol might fall on them at any time of day or night.

31   Shattered houses on the Kohima battlefield. (AB/AWH)

Although Commonwealth troops enjoyed major material advantages over the Japanese in terms of armour, air support and artillery – and a huge advantage in ammunition supply and radio communication – much of this was negated by the terrain and weather, and by the close proximity of the enemy forces. Often there would be only a short distance between the frontline troops and the cover afforded by the forest canopy; and the torrential rain frequently made observation with guns or the provision of air support by fighter-bombers of the RAF and RIAF virtually impossible.

Equally, the rain did hamper the Japanese as well. The downpours had much the same dispiriting influence and exacerbated the challenge of getting ammunition and food to the outposts, but at least the majority of the men were under cover – though it made strongpoints and bunkers prone to a degree of flooding.

General Grover's division did not fully concentrate at Dimapur until 11 April, though elements were probing Japanese dispositions by the 9th. His general plan intended not simply to eject the Japanese from Kohima, but to pin 31st Division in the

32 Commonwealth troops on the march. (AB/AWH)

mountains and destroy them completely. To this end, he planned
to send 4th Brigade (Brig. Goschen) to the south of the Japanese
line while 6th Brigade (Brig. Shapland) pressed in the centre to
dislodge the enemy from Kohima Ridge and 5th Brigade (Brig.
Hawkins) moved to cover the Japanese from the north.

The point unit of 5th Brigade reached the Kohima to Merema
road on 18 April and were followed by the rest of the brigade
over the next week. This proved to be an exhausting manoeuvre,
but one that was achieved without loss, and by the late evening
of 26 April Hawkins' force had concentrated on Merema Ridge
and was preparing to advance on the Japanese positions.

While the Commonwealth troops faced a major challenge in assembling and moving to suitable locations for the coming battle, the Japanese commander had problems of his own. The volume of supplies he had been promised for the campaign – a minimum of 10 tons per day had failed to materialise and he now faced additional demands on his depleted force. Early on 21 April a lone Japanese NCO was shot off his bicycle on the Merema road and was found to be bearing orders that 1st Battalion of 138th Regiment was to disengage, pass to the south of Kohima and march to join 15th Division in the battle at Imphal. These instructions had already been received by Gen. Sato, although he had made no effort to fulfil his instructions. Sato's division had suffered heavy casualties in the Kohima fighting and if he were to achieve any of his objectives – the most important of which was really to take Dimapur, though he had chosen to focus his efforts on Kohima – he could hardly hope to do so if his strength was reduced at all, let alone by a margin of one out of his nine infantry battalions. In addition to losses on the battlefield, his command was now struggling with food shortages, which in turn made his men more susceptible to disease. Although 31st Division had brought several large heads of cattle to provide beef on the hoof, the majority – perhaps in excess of 80 per cent – of the animals had died during the march to Kohima through exhaustion, dehydration or in falls from precipitous mountain paths. The lack of beef forced units to slaughter their mules for food, which in turn reduced their ability to secure food, medicines and ammunition from the available stores. By the time the division approached Kohima, many of the troops had contracted malaria and many more were suffering from dysentery.

His repeated demands for resupply met with refusal and it was now abundantly clear that he could not hope to renew the attack on Kohima, let alone advance on Dimapur, despite the fact that a successful attack on the latter was crucial to any remaining hopes of a major Japanese victory.

Relief

1944	23 April	General Sato orders an all-out assault on Kohima. This fails and he reconfigures his dispositions to deny the Imphal Road to Commonwealth forces
	25–29 April	2nd Division manoeuvres to destroy 31st Division and complete the relief of Kohima

The rational course of action would have been to attempt to preserve his manpower by making a withdrawal across the Chindwin River. However, Sato could not take such a course without orders and was, therefore, left with no choice but to settle his men into the mountains and jungle for a protracted defensive battle. A desperate assault on Garrison Hill during the night of 23/24 April failed to make any progress and, from that point onward, the Commonwealth troops seemed to be facing the prospect of rooting out Japanese positions one by one in a battle that would last for several more weeks.

Grover's planned encirclement of Sato's 31st Division inevitably made slow progress given the nature of the countryside and the tenacity of the Japanese soldier, many of whom had long abandoned any hope of returning to their homes and had nothing more to live for other than inflicting as much damage as they could on their opponents. The traditions of the Japanese Army conditioned soldiers to reject the idea of surrender, and army propaganda told them that the British and Indian troops facing them would kill prisoners out of hand, so the only choices were fight or flight.

The Japanese soldier, like any other, was perfectly capable of running away, but at Kohima it would have been hard to identify anywhere to run away to. If a man chose to desert his post he was faced with retracing the steps of 31st Division back to the Chindwin, through some of the most difficult terrain in the world and with every chance of being tracked down and killed by Naga hunters. If he chose to obey his orders, he would be behaving in an honourable and soldierly fashion, would benefit from whatever rations and ammunition 31st Division could acquire and be among his comrades, whereas even if he successfully negotiated his way back to the Chindwin and rejoined the army there, he would almost certainly face execution for desertion.

By 26 April 6th Brigade had their hands full on Kohima Ridge and had to withstand another attempt on Kuki Piquet, which was successfully driven off at considerable cost to both sides. The attack had been abandoned by dawn at which point two companies of the Dorsets was able to mount an attack which made some progress against the Japanese bunkers, but was impeded by the torrential rain and the fierce determination of the enemy. The attack did, however, allow two troops of tanks (Grants from 149th Regiment and Stuarts from 45th Cavalry) and a party of Royal Engineers in Bren Carriers to force their way through the enemy positions to join 5th Brigade for the loss of one tank.

33   Commonwealth troops manning a light anti-tank gun. (AB/AWH)

The progress of 4th Brigade was slow. Although a small number of tanks had been brought into the fight, the terrain was just too difficult for the infantry to get forward under fire. After a failed attempt to seize Firs Hill, Gen. Grover decided that the best use of the brigade was to prevent 31st Division from reinforcing their surviving troops on Kohima Ridge from the north.

By the next day, Grover had developed a new plan. His 4th Brigade, in conjunction with 161st Brigade, would block the Imphal road by taking the Aradura Spur and attack the remaining Japanese forces on GPT Ridge from the south and west. At the same time 5th Brigade would seize the Naga village, thus squeezing the Japanese from two directions, while 6th Brigade would attack FSD Hill with armoured support and then press on to Jail Hill.

34   *Airstrike on a Japanese supply train. (AB/AWH)*

The Final Onslaught

| | 30 April | Grover's 4th Brigade re-establishes lines of communication from Jotsoma to Kohima |
| 1944 | 5 May | Armoured attack successfully ejects Japanese forces from FSD Hill, but with heavy losses |

By 30 April it had become apparent that the Japanese still had considerable strength on GPT Ridge and the Aradura Spur, and there was little chance of forcing them out of both positions simultaneously with the forces available. Grover now assigned 4th Brigade to an attack on GPT Ridge. It was expected that this could not be mounted until 5 May due to the extreme difficulties of moving the brigade on foot, but the 2nd Norfolks were able to take up positions there on the 4th and, with 4/1st Ghurkhas, now managed to establish a clear line of communications back to Jotsoma. The remaining Japanese troops on Kuki Piquet were now very nearly encircled, though they continued to fight with incredible determination. The following day a force of nine Grant and five Stuart tanks tried to force their way to FSD Hill with the intention of consolidating the progress made on the 4th, but, although various engineering stores were delivered, this was only achieved at some cost and five of the Grants were put out of action, effectively blocking the main road.

Meanwhile, 6th Brigade had not been able to take Jail Hill and the remaining reserve unit, 1st Queen's Royal Regiment, was committed to the task early on 7 May. Initially they made good progress, but the Queen's were brought to a halt when they encountered a particularly strong bunker complex at the top of the hill which was amply supported with fire from the enemy positions on DIS Hill and GPT Ridge. The attack was eventually abandoned by mid-afternoon and the unit withdrew under cover of a heavy smoke screen.

35   A Fourteenth Army observation post directing artillery fire. (AB/AWH)

36   British troops at Kohima. (Author's collection)

Elsewhere there had been some progress throughout the day. 6th Brigade managed to establish themselves firmly on FDS Hill and was pressing on with clearing the DC's bungalow, but the eastern aspects of Kuki Piquet and FSD Hill still remained in enemy hands and could call on fire support from other positions. 5th Brigade had been able to achieve a firm grip on the western edge of the Naga village but had not been able to clear it.

There was now something of a lull in the battle, though it can hardly have been apparent to the troops on the ground, whether Commonwealth or Japanese, due to the continued shelling, sniping and patrol activities. In the absence of major attacks, both sides were able to concentrate their efforts on stockpiling and distributing supplies and – for the Japanese – preparing their dug-outs and trenches for the next onslaught.

Early on 11 May, Brig. Loftus-Tottenham's 33rd Brigade, with 1st Queen's and 4/15th Punjab leading, and with 4/1 Ghurkha in reserve, advanced toward DIS Hill and Jail Hill, while 5th Brigade renewed its attack through the Naga village as 4th and 6th Brigade continued the process of destroying the Japanese positions on the southern aspects of FSD ridge and Kuki Piquet.

Although 33rd Brigade's advance made a promising start, by 0700hrs it had been brought to a halt in front of strongly held Japanese entrenchments by devastatingly accurate fire from the reverse slope of GPT Ridge and FSD Ridge. A squadron of Grant tanks from 149th Royal Armoured Corps (RAC), which had been tasked with supporting the attack on FSD Ridge, found they could not get past a roadblock which the Japanese had constructed around the four tanks that had been lost nearly a week before. As the day wore on it became apparent that little more progress could be made and a vast concentration of smoke was deployed so that casualties could be evacuated. Then, at about 1900hrs, a mist descended on the battlefield, obscuring the Commonwealth troops from fire and allowing them to dig in close to the Japanese positions while food and ammunition was brought up to them.

By around 1030hrs the following day the roadblock of disabled tanks had been removed and the balance of the tank squadron was able to come to the support of 33rd Brigade who were now able to make a slow but steady advance over the course of the day. Meanwhile 4th and 5th Brigades, despite hard fighting, remained more or less stalled to the north and south. Therefore, when night fell there were still Japanese troops ensconced on Jail Hill and DIS Ridge, and in trenches and foxholes stretching from Jail Hill to Kuki Piquet, but by dawn on the following day 33rd Brigade had finally broken the spirit of the defenders and were able to inflict heavy casualties as they abandoned one position after another. The remaining bunkers around the DC's bungalow held out for a while, but a determined push by the Dorsets eventually destroyed the last remnants of the Japanese forces on Kohima Ridge.

The units of 33rd Brigade and 2nd Division could now receive supplies and replacements, but the Kohima battle was not yet complete. General Sato's 31st division was extremely short of food and ammunition, battlefield casualties had been heavy and many more men had been lost to illness, but it was still a potent force and could still shell the Kohima to Imphal road. By 24 May 5th Brigade had been relieved at the Naga village by 33rd Brigade, thus allowing Grover to reunite 2nd Division and go on to the offensive. Their advance began on 27 May with an attempt by 6th Brigade to seize Aradura Hill with 4th and 5th Brigade in support advancing in parallel on either side of the main road while an armoured column pushed along the road between them. The attack did not fare well; a Japanese unit made an audacious local counter-attack and – probably by sheer chance – captured the 6th Brigade tactical HQ. At much the same time the tanks encountered a minefield which proved to be very difficult to neutralise and heavy casualties were incurred by the engineers. A further attack by 1st Royal Scots and 2nd Norfolks fared no better and was abandoned by about 1630hrs with nothing to show for it but heavy losses.

Meanwhile, 33rd Brigade was still engaged at the Naga village. On 30 and 31 May, 4/15th Punjab and 4/1st Ghurkhas made repeated attacks to little avail and with heavy losses, with one company of the Punjabs being reduced to only eighteen men. Although they had made little ground, they had inflicted considerable loss on the enemy and, after dusk on 1 June, an attack by 1st Queen's under cover of the evening mist entered the Naga village to find it empty – the Japanese had withdrawn earlier in the day.

At Aradura Ridge the Commonwealth troops continued to be held up by small, but utterly determined, groups of Japanese soldiers, often no more than a section or platoon of men, but well protected in carefully sited bunkers and trenches. However brave and committed they might be, the Japanese soldiers were in a hopeless position. Whether through lack of ammunition or simply a matter of accepting the inevitable, the last Japanese troops had withdrawn during the night of 3/4 June; 1st Assam Regiment took possession of Pulebadze and, after a brief show of resistance by a small Japanese rearguard, 5th Brigade captured Phesama Ridge.

General Sato's 31st Division had been beaten decisively, but were still in remarkably good order for a formation that had travelled through such hard countryside, endured such harsh conditions, suffered such heavy casualties and failed to achieve its objectives. Once it became clear that he could not hope to complete the capture of Kohima nor press on to Dimapur, Sato's objective became the obstruction of the Commonwealth drive to relieve Imphal. In this he had achieved an incredible degree of success, especially bearing in mind his dreadful supply situation and his heavy losses in battle and to disease. He had failed to destroy the Kohima garrison, but he had stopped 2nd Division in its attacks at Aradura and forced 33rd Brigade to a standstill at the Naga village, and clearly there was a limit to what his troops could do. On 31 May he arranged to leave elements of

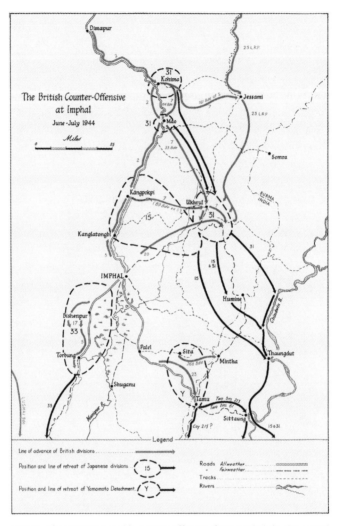

Map 6   The Commonwealth counter-offensive from Imphal. (Butler, p.352)

124th and 138th Regiments in and around the Naga village and ordered his senior infantry commander, Gen. Miyazaki, to form a rearguard of about 600 men to hold up the Allies at Aradura. These units would either die in their trenches or, in due course – if at all possible – disengage and follow the balance of the division as it made its escape across country, abandoning much of what remained of their equipment. Sato's 15th Division was more than beaten; it was close to utter destruction.

AFTER THE BATTLE

General Sato's 31st Division had not only failed to achieve the objectives of the operation, it had been all but destroyed as a viable fighting force. While they were meeting disaster at Kohima, the rest of the great U-Go offensive was unravelling with similar consequences for the rest of the Burma Area Army. At the beginning of the campaign, Gen. Scoones' IV Corps had been poised for an offensive of its own, and was not, therefore, ideally deployed for defence. Fearing that the forward elements could become isolated and be defeated in detail, Gen. Slim authorised Gen. Scoones to withdraw to the Imphal plain, thus shortening the Allied lines of communication while the Japanese logistic effort came under increasing strain because of the distances involved, the harsh country and because of interdiction missions flown by the RAF and RIAF.

Concentrating his forces at Imphal allowed Slim and Scoones the opportunity to fight a major battle on their own terms. Commonwealth troops had found that they increasingly had the edge on the Japanese in battle in the jungle and now that they were fighting on the plain, their air combat support, their artillery and their armour were all much more effective than in previous encounters.

37   A view of the shell-scarred Kohima battlefield. (AB/AWH)

Once the battle was flowing in the Allies' favour, and the enemy were in retreat, there was no place where Japanese forces could make a properly coordinated stand which would allow Mutaguchi an opportunity to regroup and reorganise his forces. The Allied advance was remorseless and every effort was made to destroy the enemy before he could get across the Chindwin to replenish and dig in. The heavy casualties incurred by the Japanese in battle were made worse by failures in supply, which meant that Japanese soldiers were dying of hunger-induced exhaustion. For the first time in the whole Burma conflict they started to surrender in sufficient numbers to give the Allies a decent intelligence picture based on more than observation and interpretation. The morale of the Burma Area Army units was battered, but by no means destroyed, and British, Indian and African troops still faced a lot of hard fighting. There was, however, clearly no realistic prospect of a Japanese recovery. Allied morale continued to improve as Japanese spirits sank and even if Gen. Mutaguchi had miraculously found a means of spiriting his troops out of harm's way and into safe quarters with ample food and medical supplies, there was no means of rebuilding his army as a fighting force. Japanese factories could not produce the guns, armour and small arms to replace those lost in battle or abandoned in the retreat, and Japanese society could not provide the manpower. Even if these things had been possible, there was no time to rain replacements and no shipping to get them into the fight.

At the start of the campaign the Burma Area Army was no longer the confident and competent force it had been in 1942, but by the end of the campaign it was a mere shadow of its former self. If the troops expected the supply situation to improve as they withdrew to their starting positions, they were to be sadly disappointed; airstrikes and sabotage operations had crippled communications all the way to the Thai border. Increasing numbers of administrative and supply troops were now redundant and were being remustered as infantry, but they had little training and – in the main – no experience of any value; many of them had no rifles and those who did had precious little ammunition.

The U-Go offensive was the only major initiative of 1944. In the Pacific theatre, Japan was on the back foot as American forces advanced from one island to another, mounting air raids against the Japanese homeland with consequent damage to industry and civilian morale. Losses to commercial shipping had mounted steadily since mid-1942 and were impossible to replace, so it was, therefore, increasingly difficult to get the limited materials that industry could produce to where it needed to be – right across a vast perimeter stretching through the Pacific and South Asia to Burma.

Defeat made the survivors less confident of eventual victory and, with declining morale from late 1944 onward, it became easier for the Commonwealth forces to take prisoners, though most Japanese soldiers were still fighting with incredible determination. Although the intelligence and planning staffs of Fourteenth Army were keen to have POWs, several factors precluded this: the determination of so many Japanese soldiers to fight on to the bitter end; the practice of having to pound each enemy position to dust to make progress; and an unwillingness among Commonwealth troops to take prisoners given the general experience of the campaign. It was common knowledge that the Japanese generally would not take POWs in Burma and, when they did, they almost invariably treated them with great cruelty – wounded men left behind in action were often murdered for sport. The situation was not much better for INA troops. Indian soldiers who had not deserted to the enemy were not inclined to have much respect for those who had.

The failure of the U-Go offensive had a political impact in Burma and India. The Japanese occupation in Burma was clearly not going to last very much longer and even elements that had been strongly opposed to colonial status before the war started to make overtures to the British with a view to being on the right side when the war came to an end. In India the British had kept close control of the media and the INA had not figured prominently, other than as renegades who had betrayed their word and who had been duped and used by the Japanese. The political subtext was that the defeat of the British would simply have meant a rather more oppressive rule from Japan, and that brave and loyal Indian soldiers had been in the forefront of a struggle to protect their country from a rapacious enemy.

The direct threat to India had been removed and the Japanese were being driven from Indian soil in Manipur. This was a major boost to pro-British sentiment. This was more important in much of India than is generally realised today; not all Indians were in favour of the Indian National Congress campaign for independence. At the time it was significant both in 'British' India and in the much larger area of the Princely States. Many people in the latter – and not just the princes themselves – were happy at the prospect of a massive Indian union imposing a single central authority on the many countries which were, at least notionally, independent of British rule.

Defeating Japan on India's borders restored some credibility for Britain as a power capable of protecting India, but so many Fourteenth Army troops were Indian that the victory also gave credibility to the proposition that India could defend herself against invasion in the future, which rather undermined one of the justifications for the continuation of British rule once the war was over.

The routes through Burma, used to carry materials to support China's drive against Japanese occupation, had been secured. As the flow of supplies increased, the Chinese forces improved in efficiency and the China front became an ever-greater strain on Japan's over-stretched resources. Cutting the Burma air and land routes had been a significant objective of the U-Go plan, but it is not clear that any great progress would have resulted. It is possible that some Japanese planners thought that depriving the Chinese armies of supplies would have reduced their effectiveness to such a degree that it would be possible to reduce the quantity of material sent to the China front, or even that it might be possible to force an armistice with China, releasing men and material for service elsewhere.

38   Battle-damaged building at Kohima. (AB/AWH)

However, this was not even close to being a realistic possibility. The Japanese occupation in China had been hideously cruel and millions of people had died. Chiang Kai-shek could not possibly make peace with Japan on any terms without destroying his own political credibility at home and abroad. The stream of material and money from America and Britain that had supported him for years would be cut off at source and he would not be able to maintain a force against his other enemy – the communists.

Although there had been a cessation of hostilities in order to focus on a common foe and free China from occupation, in practice the communists had done very little fighting against the invader and had instead concentrated on building up their strength and consolidating their power in regions which they had already seized from Chiang Kai-shek's government. However hard the struggle, Chiang Kai-shek could never make peace with Japan for fear that he would then cede a moral authority to Mao's communists who would then claim to be China's bastion against foreign aggression.

Even if this unlikely prospect of a Chinese armistice had occurred, Japan would need large forces in China to protect gains made in the past or abandon them to the enemy, which would be bad for the prestige of the Government, the morale of the civilians at home and the armed services overseas. Even if it had proved possible to cut the Burma routes entirely, the reality was that Chiang Kai-shek would not make peace. China had fought Japan for more than a decade with precious little help from outside until 1941. The best that could be hoped for in that quarter was that the Chinese armies, deprived of ammunition, might have to reduce their activity to a point where the Japanese forces in China could reduce their demands on Japan's economy, though there was little chance that that reduction would be sufficient to make any real difference to the situation in any other theatre.

The defeat of Operations U-Go did, however, give a certain impetus to Chinese forces, particularly those in northern Burma.

A growing belief that victory could be gained sooner rather than later improved morale and the passage of supplies became easier, allowing more ambitious and effective operations in both China and Burma.

The defeat in Burma had consequences back in Japan. Thousands upon thousands of families received that their sons were missing in action and most must have realised that the overwhelming majority had been killed. The opening stages of the campaign had been widely broadcast, so failure – in the only major offensive for a year – was another indication that any hope of a final victory was fast slipping away. The losses in men and equipment could not possibly be made good and the assets of Burma – which had never been fully available to Japan even at the height of the occupation – would now fall to the enemy. Worse still, however much the Japanese occupation governments in Malaya and the Dutch East Indies tried to obscure the defeat, the British did their utmost to ensure that people under Japanese occupation were made aware of the victory.

In Malaya, the events of March–July 1944 did a great deal to enhance the standing of the Malayan people's Anti-Japanese Army (MPAJA) and foster confidence that the British would return and drive the Japanese from the peninsula. The MPAJA had grown out of disparate groups opposed to the occupation and a liberal dusting of bandits looking for opportunities. It was largely centred on the Chinese community to begin with, but the oppressive nature of the occupation had brought recruits from the indigenous Malay population and from the Indian community. Despite the largely communist nature of the MPAJA, it had received arms, money and training from British sources and, by mid-1944, was starting to become a real problem for the Japanese administration. The support was offered as a means of carrying the fight to the enemy, but also as a declaration of intent – that the British had every intention of regaining control over the colony she had lost in 1942.

The majority of MPAJA members, however, had a rather different objective – to gain independence from British rule once the Japanese had been defeated. Before the war, independence had not really been a major issue for a number of reasons, but now there was a considerable overlap between nationalist and communist sentiment. Before the war, many of the nationalist activists and the overwhelming majority of the communists were Chinese, and most of the remainder were Indians. The native Malayan community had initially taken little part in either group in the 1920s and 1930s, but had become more inclined toward independence during the war years, partly in reaction to the failure of the British to provide an adequate defence against aggression and partly as a result of the nature of the Japanese occupation. Although the occupation had – as a rule – been much more aggressive to the Chinese community and had, to some extent, left the Malays in peace, the decline in trade and industry and the requisition of agricultural produce for the Japanese military had led to widespread poverty and hunger. As a result nationalist sympathy had increased markedly.

Malaya was really a blanket term for a collection of colonies and states. Under British control there had been three separate categories of administration – the Federated Malay States, the Unfederated Malay States and Straits Settlements. Increasingly, the prospect of uniting all of these into a single country that could furnish its own defence was gaining popularity, even if the general view was that it would take a British invasion to get the Japanese out first. By the time the invasion force – Operation Zipper – landed, the war had come to an end. The atomic bombs had forced the Japanese Government to surrender, though there was no guarantee that the Japanese forces in Malaya would not fight on regardless of the Emperor's instructions. When it became clear that they would not – and that may only have been because their commander, Field Marshal Terauchi, had a heart attack and could not pursue the campaign of resistance that he had intended – the

MPAJA either laid down their arms or hid them away for a time when they might be used against the British. The 'emergency' that broke out in Malaya in 1948 and continued until after independence was not a simple consequence of the defeat of the Japanese in Burma, but the growth of the MPAJA in 1944–45 was, in part at least, a product of increasing confidence that Malaya, like Burma, would be liberated from the Japanese.

Numerous individuals saw their reputations suffer as a result of the failure of Operation U-Go. Prime Minster Hideki Tojo was not forced to resign until the fall of Saipan in July 1944, but defeat in the India-Burma theatre meant that his days were already numbered. Although he had authorised the operation, Gen. Kawabe was not officially held personally responsible and his replacement in August 1944 by Gen. Kimura was on the grounds of ill-health, not incompetence. General Mutaguchi had lost all credibility – as well as 50,000 Japanese soldiers –and was forced into retirement at the end of the year. It was put to Gen. Sato that he should commit suicide for his failure to take Kohima and Dimapur, but instead

39   *Chinese and American drivers on the Burma Road. (AB/AWH)*

MULTICULTURALISM

Although the word is modern, the meaning was well understood by General Slim, who was determined to assure Indian, African, Nepalese and Chinese soldiers that they were just as valued as their British comrades. Building an effective army out of the wide array of racial, linguistic and cultural components of Fourteenth Army was an incredible, and often overlooked, achievement.

he demanded a formal court martial so that he could defend his honour and his professional reputation. This might not have been a wise move since he had essentially failed to pursue the main objective – the supply depots and railhead at Dimapur – but had allowed himself to become fixated on what was really a subsidiary operation – the capture of Kohima. Anxious to avoid a difficult trial, Gen. Kawabe arranged for Sato to be declared unfit to stand trial.

The Burma Area Army had suffered massive casualties, lost much of its equipment and was fatally injured as a fighting force, but had nothing to show for the sacrifices made. The defeat of 1944 overshadows the exceptional achievements of the Japanese forces in 1942–43: the fragile and tenuous supply lines, inadequate and insufficient equipment, the determination of the soldiers, and the skills and audacity of Japanese commanders are all forgotten in the wake of defeat. It is all too easy to forget that even U-Go – an immensely risky undertaking – came quite close to bringing a major victory over the Commonwealth forces.

It is not certain that British rule in India could have withstood a Japanese victory in April 1944. General Mutaguchi's view that a successful offensive would bring about a general uprising against the British throughout India was, at best, highly speculative and optimistic, but equally it was not impossible. Even a relatively minor increase in resistance to colonial rule would have been further challenge to the British Government and the Government of India at a time when there were already enormous demands on their resources. Additionally, a major outbreak of unrest in India might, conceivably, have stimulated anti-British feeling throughout the Empire and in countries which, although not strictly speaking part of the British establishment themselves, were under British occupation, such as Persia (Iran) and Egypt.

Wherever there are losers, there are generally winners too. There had been widespread doubt about the appointment of Lord Mountbatten as the Supreme Commander of SEAC, particularly in senior British Army circles. He had been seen as a dilettante promoted on the basis of his connections, but the critics were – largely – now silenced. The 1944 campaign gave him credibility and he became popular with his troops, despite his class and background. He understood that the men needed more than food, fuel and ammunition and was generally seen as doing his best by the men under his command. His commitment to decent treatment for the Indian forces also helped to give him credibility when he was appointed viceroy.

The campaign confirmed Gen. Slim as one of the great commanders of the Second World War. His efforts to ensure the general well-being of the troops, as well as bringing victory, made him one of the most popular British commanders of all time. He had turned around the fortunes of the army after nearly two years of defeat and frustration – partly by ensuring that the troops got everything that he could procure and partly by making the army healthier. In 1943 illness had been nearly one hundred times more damaging than battlefield casualties, with malaria the major scourge. Many soldiers avoided taking their mepacrine (anti-malarial) tablets so that they could contract malaria and be sent to hospitals in India, far away from the front. Slim ensured that malaria cases were retained in Forward Treatment Units (FTU) so that they could be returned to their units as soon as possible – the malaria rate decreased rapidly. It also did no harm that soldiers soon became aware that Slim would cheerfully sack senior officers who failed to come up to the mark. He believed strongly in the equality of every soldier in the army, regardless of race or culture, at a time when such views were not popular.

South East Asia Command as a whole – and the 'forgotten' Fourteenth Army in particular – gained in confidence and self-esteem. The war in the Far East was still overshadowed by events in Europe, and all the more so after the Normandy landings on 6 June 1944, the breakout battles and the race across France and into Belgium. The battles raging in Europe, therefore, kept the war in the Far East off the front pages at the time. In the decades that have passed, historians have been guilty of allowing the Burma war – indeed the Asian war in general – to remain something of a backwater. The trials and tribulations of the British, Indian and African men and women of SEAC and the horrendous suffering of Asian communities under Japanese occupation have been largely ignored. Few people are aware that three entire African divisions and various African ancillary units served with distinction in this distant and arduous conflict.

Among the 'winners' of the war in the Far East, we might include the many senior figures whose poor analysis, lack of interest and – in some cases – a more-or-less wilful failure to give serious thought to the potential risk of Japanese invasions in Burma and Malaya brought about so much unnecessary suffering. Defeat in Burma in 1942 is sometimes blamed on local commanders, despite them having totally inadequate resources to deal with the threat, while the senior figures who had failed to make adequate preparations managed to avoid responsibility completely.

The focus on European and British affairs has also had an impact on perceptions of the Pacific war. The desperate struggles of Australasian and American forces on land and sea is not widely appreciated, despite their crucial significance in the war against Japan and, therefore, to the war effort generally. Much the same applies to the efforts of China. Chiang Kai-shek's forces fought against Japanese conquest and occupation for more

40   Battlefield defoliation. (AB/AWH)

than a decade, but they also had to contend with Mao and the communists who used war to further their domestic position. Chinese troops have often been denigrated or simply ignored, but they were a vital part of the Burma campaign and, therefore, of the war in the Far East as a whole. Without the sacrifice of the Chinese troops, there would have been many more Japanese to fight against Commonwealth forces and the outcome might well have been radically different; an outright Japanese victory in 1943 would have altered the whole course of the war in the East and might have brought about the very anti-British uprising throughout India that Gen. Mutaguchi hoped to achieve in 1944.

The majority of the Kohima garrison consisted of Indian, Nepalese Army and Ghurkha troops, but their gallant and conscientious contribution has been rather forgotten due to the perception – encouraged, perhaps, by Arthur Campbell's novel *The Siege: A Story from Kohima* – that the RWK fought almost alone.

The Battle of Kohima was not fought in isolation. While the garrison there were fighting valiantly, the other units of

161st Brigade – 1/1st Punjab and 4/7th Rajputs – were surrounded 2 miles (3.2km) away at Jotsoma. Their battle has attracted much less attention, perhaps because it was less obviously dramatic. It is also too easy to forget that the end of the siege was not the end of the battle. The Japanese went on to the defensive, but still had to be driven out of Kohima and away from the surrounding hills and mountain if the Dimapur–Imphal road was to return to full capacity. The brigades of Gen. Grover's 2nd Division had a long and hard fight to finish the job.

Kohima very nearly fell to the Japanese, and surely would have done had it not been for the exemplary conduct of several units in the week or more before the commencement of the siege. The Assam Regiment, despite the fact that most of the men were still new to army life, let alone combat, fought with exceptional skill and tenacity, as did 50th Indian Parachute Brigade at Sangshak. The steadfast service of all of these units has received little attention and even less recognition, but without it the Kohima story and, therefore, that of the great battle at Imphal, might have had a very different ending.

Among the beneficiaries was the political establishment of British India. Preventing any further Japanese penetration into India was certainly good for British prestige and helped to promote a case that the British were both willing and able to protect India from foreign aggression, and driving them out of India and then through Burma showed that the British were still a powerful military force. General Slim's victory – and it was very much Slim's abilities that had made victory a reality rather than a possibility – helped the civil administration to weather the storms of Mahatma Ghandi's 'quit India' campaign and general civil unrest, especially in Bengal where there had been a serious famine in 1943 leading to millions of deaths. The famine had arisen from a poor rice crop in 1942, followed by tidal waves, cyclones and a fungus that may have destroyed more rice than the waves and the cyclones put together. It was also, in part, a consequence of the Japanese

41 Japanese prisoners of war. Very few Japanese soldiers surrendered until the later stages of the campaign in 1945. (AB/AWH)

invasion of Burma since a large proportion of the Burmese rice crop was normally exported to Calcutta.

Another beneficiary was the cause of Burmese nationalism. The welcome that the Japanese had received in some quarters at the start of the war waned as it became increasingly clear that Japan was not an ally against British colonialism, but the source of an oppressive occupation. This became more evident in the latter stages of the occupation, since there was no longer any thought at all as to the long-term political consequences of exploitation; by late 1943 the occupation was simply a matter of undisguised asset-stripping to support the Japanese war effort. Disenchantment with the Japanese led to dialogue with the British and, eventually, the Burmese puppet government declared war on Japan to ensure a role in any post-war negotiations on independence. In practice, Burmese independence was not really in doubt, though the hurried nature of dismantling the colonial relationship was a major factor in bringing about a long and cruel Burmese civil war after independence.

The Naga people were, arguably, the greatest losers in the long term. Many were killed and much collateral damage incurred simply by the war passing through their country, and many were pressed into transporting supplies for the Japanese Army. Their crops and livestock were stolen, there was widespread abuse, rape and murder, and the destruction of entire villages for being uncooperative. The Nagas were, at best, suspicious of future government under the Burmese majority of the plains and cities, and they feared marginalisation, loss of territory and the loss of traditional rights and practices which were long protected by the British.

THE LEGACY

The impact and legacy of the wider campaign in which the siege and battle of Kohima was a crucial action was considerable, though not necessarily immediately apparent. In simple operational terms it was certainly a significant turning point in the fortunes of the Commonwealth forces in Burma and, therefore, in the course of the war in Asia as a whole. Equally, it was rather more than just a costly battlefield defeat for the Japanese Army – significant as that was. The Japanese had been beaten in the past: their defeat by the Soviet Union in 1939 had not passed unnoticed among the European powers, but nor was it seen as a clash of first-rate armies. The Russians were not widely admired for their military abilities and there was a view that if the Russians had beaten Japan then the Japanese really were not a major threat, at least in terms of warfare on land.

The hard-fought successes won by the Americans in the island campaigns of the Pacific drew little attention in the United Kingdom compared to the campaign in Italy – understandably given the relative proximity and the far greater involvement of Commonwealth troops – but the circumstances were rather different as well. The Pacific battles were seen, not altogether realistically, as assaults on prepared positions rather than as battles of manoeuvre.

42   Devastated buildings immediately after the battle. (AB/AWH)

The defeat of the U-Go offensive, to most people anyway, was the first time the Japanese had been thoroughly defeated on a grand scale. It destroyed forever the reputation of the Imperial Japanese Army as masters of jungle warfare, though this had, in fact, been something of a myth in the first place. More generally, the campaign of 1944 demonstrated that the tide of the war had most certainly turned against Japan and that outright victory, though still some way in the distance, was at least possible.

Although the Japanese authorities in the occupied countries endeavoured to keep news of the defeat out of the public domain, information inevitably seeped through and this gave encouragement to the resistance forces and undermined morale among Japanese servicemen on land and sea.

Defeat in Burma was a further blow to Japan's waning political authority. The concept of Japan's Greater Asia Co-Prosperity Sphere, promoting the economic and cultural unity of the East Asian race, had never really had much credibility, even in the heady days of success, and by 1944 was widely discredited. Later, in the wake of the defeats at Imphal and Kohima, it became quite meaningless. The Government of Thailand was no longer confident of Japan establishing herself as the primary power in the Far East and the political relationship between the two countries began to deteriorate rapidly. Although the Japanese occupation in the Netherlands East Indies had manage to establish a more positive relationship with the people than anywhere else in the extended empire, it was becoming clear that she was going to lose the war. Japanese promises of granting some form of notional independence now lost any remaining credibility and nationalist politicians, administrators and activists started to look toward establishing their independence from the Netherlands as soon as the Japanese were defeated.

In Burma itself, the already poor relationships between the different racial, religious and cultural communities – the Anglo-Indians, Anglo-Burmese, the Burmese of the plains and towns, and the different hill peoples – were not improved by the experience of the war. Resentment of the Anglo-Burmese, the Indians and the Anglo-Indians – and of course of the British themselves – had fostered support for Japan in the early stages of the invasion and occupation in 1942. Japanese behaviour as an essentially colonialist power had largely destroyed such sympathies, but had encouraged Burmese people to believe that they should not accept colonial rule from any quarter, but should look forward to administering their own affairs.

Given the extent of nationalist activity over the preceding half a century and more, and the fact that there had been a degree of acceptance or even welcome for the Japanese, it should have been clear to the British that colonial rule in Burma could not last for long once the war was over. However, a lot of former residents – people who had made their careers in the civil administration or in business – seem to have thought that they would be able to pick up their lives where they had left them at the time of the invasion. Clearly this could not be the case and negotiations were under way with nationalist politicians before the war had ended, who, naturally enough, were largely representative of the majority of the population, the people of the great central plains and the towns and cities.

On the other hand, the British were now rather more suspicious of 'plains' Burmese and more sympathetic to the Nagas, Chins and Karens who had, in the main, been more supportive of the Commonwealth forces. In turn the wider Burmese community had some cause to feel that the British had failed to protect them from invasion, and nationalist sentiment, which had always been more significant than in most British colonies, came to the fore as the only really important political issue in post-war Burma.

The hill peoples had proved – largely – to be better disposed to the British than the mainstream of Burmese society. This was partly due to the work of respected sympathetic personalities like Charles Pawsey and people like the guerrilla leader Ursula Graham Bower, but also to a perception that British rule offered a degree of protection from the wider community. Subsequent events indicate that this may have been correct, but after the war Britain was not in a position to deny Burmese independence even had she wanted to. She might have made an effort to erect a separate state, or several states, down the mountain chain that separated Burma from India, but it is unlikely that such an arrangement would have survived.

1944 effectively ended any prospect that the Indian National Army could become a major factor in bringing about independence for India. Japan had never really made much effort to turn the INA into a real force and could no longer find enough small arms to keep the INA in the fight. As a result, morale crumbled and the majority of INA troops surrendered to Commonwealth forces without much of a struggle. One winner in that connection was Subhas Chandra Bose, who somehow managed to become a hero of the independence movement, though in fact he was little more than a self-seeking tool of the Japanese. It is widely believed that he died in an aircraft crash in Taiwan in 1945, though there is some doubt about this. He certainly did not re-surface after partition (the separation of India and Pakistan) and Indian independence, as might have been expected had he survived

Service in the Commonwealth forces, and most particularly in the Burma war where whole divisions were deployed, may have gone some way to encouraging nationalist sentiment among African soldiers. The large numbers of African officers who developed an ability to lead and inspire doubtless made a significant contribution to the drive for independence in British African colonies after the war.

The situation in Burma in mid-1945 can be seen as an indication that European colonialism in Asia was coming to an end. British defeat at the hands of Japan had undermined confidence in the power and permanency of the 'raj' and Japanese defeat at the hands of the Commonwealth forces had utterly destroyed the credibility of Japan as an imperial power. The British might have returned to power, but it was already self-evident that they were not altogether welcome.

If the British were coming to the end of their days as a power in Burma, the same applied in India. It was clear that Indian soldiers had carried much of the burden of the campaign from the very start and this encouraged the belief that India could protect herself against foreign powers and, therefore, did not need the protection of the British Empire.

In Burma, the Indian Army and Indian Air Force came of age as something rather more than elements in the defence structure of the British Empire, and this had an impact that has drawn little comment from historians. It is not widely understood that many thousands of ostensibly 'British' people effectively saw themselves as Indian. It was perfectly possible for a 'British' family to have had no real connection with Britain for a century and more. Many families – long resident in India – sent their children to get an education 'back home' and that might be the only experience those individuals ever had with their nominal place of origin; others simply went to school in India. A large proportion of both groups made their careers and spent their lives in India – in the army, the civil service or in business – and married into similar families with only the most tenuous links to the United Kingdom. A lot of these individuals experienced considerable prejudice as being 'too Indian' and many thousands elected to stay on in India after independence; indeed, many army officers, even before the war, described themselves as 'Indian' rather than 'British'.

This is exemplified by the account – possibly apocryphal – of a senior officer of the Indian Army at a conference. On hearing a speaker talk of the importance of defeating Japan as part of the overall defence of Britain, he remarked that, as far as he was concerned, the purpose of the war was to drive the Japanese out of his country – India. He claimed to have no great interest in the fortunes of the United Kingdom and went on to say that his father had once visited Britain in the days before the Great War and had thought it was a 'miserable shit of a place'.

If the war undermined Britain as a colonial power, which it most assuredly did, there is an argument that of all the victorious nations of the Second World War, India – and, therefore, modern-day Pakistan – gained least for the most effort. Millions of Indian soldiers served in Malaya, Burma, Singapore, Egypt, Tunisia, Libya, Algeria, East Africa, Persia and Italy in the struggle against fascism. In terms of blood, produce and money, India had paid a huge price but did not have a presence at the peace negotiations once the war was over, unlike France which had been defeated in 1940. The war certainly hastened the unification of India and Pakistan into one country, though without the war it might have been possible to achieve unification without the wars that have occurred since then. The formation of the Indian Union and of Pakistan came at the expense of the independent princes, but possibly prevented an extended war across the subcontinent which may or may not still have resulted in the Indian Union or something very similar.

43   The Kohima Memorial. (AB/AWH)

Unquestionably, the Second World War helped to increase the numbers of Indian officers and hastened the formation of the Royal Indian Air Force. Established in 1932, development of the RIAF had been slow, with only three squadrons formed at the outbreak of war in 1939, though numerous Indian personnel served with RAF squadrons throughout Bomber, Fighter and Coastal Commands in North Africa and in Europe. By the end of the war there were seven operational squadrons and at least one squadron – No. 7, commanded by Squadron Leader Hem Chaudhuri, equipped with the Hurribomber and based at Uderband Airstrip – made sorties at Kohima. These units became the nucleus of the Indian Air Force when the military establishment of the Republics of India and Pakistan came into being in 1947.

Indian independence was a catalyst for nationalist movements across the world, not just those in the British Empire. If self-government was achievable for India then it was achievable for Malaya, Indo-China, Indonesia, Kenya and scores of other nations which had been subject to – and in some cases formed by – colonial rule from Europe. In little more than thirty years after 1945, there was hardly a formal colonial possession anywhere in the world. In hindsight – because it was by no means obvious at the time – all of this was inevitable, but the process was unquestionably hastened by the experience and political outcomes of the Second World War. The campaign in Burma and the Battle of Kohima were a significant part of that story.

ORDERS OF BATTLE

The Kohima garrison, Commonwealth forces (Colonel Richards)

None of the units below was present in any great strength – in some cases only a platoon or a company – so the garrison consisted of elements of these battalions and men of the RASC, RE, RIASC and many other corps and departments of the British and Indian Armies. An excellent detailed order of battle for the entirety of General Stopford's XXXIII Corps can be found in Robert Lyman's *Kohima 1944*.

1st Assam Regiment
3/2nd Punjab
1st Garrison Battalion, Burma Regiment
5th Burma Regiment
27/5th Mahratta Light Infantry
3rd Assam Rifles
Shere Regiment, Nepalese Army
1432 Company Indian Army Pioneer Corps
80th Light Field Ambulance

161st Indian Brigade (Brig. Warren)

The Royal West Kents fought their battle as part of the garrison of Kohima, but were one of the units of 161st Brigade.

4th Royal West Kents
1/1st Punjab
4/7th Rajputs

31st Division, Imperial Japanese Army (General Sato)

58th Infantry Regiment (three battalions)
124th Infantry Regiment (three battalions)
138th Infantry Regiment (three battalions)
31st Mountain Artillery Regiment (three battalions)

FURTHER READING

A great many books on the Battle of Kohima have been published, but it is important to see the action in the wider setting of the campaign of 1944 and of the Burma war as a whole, so this brief list includes volumes which will give the reader a more complete picture of the war in the Far East, as well as a more detailed understanding of the Kohima situation.

Allen, Louis, *The Longest War* (1984)
Colvin, John, *Not Ordinary Men* (1994)
Edwards, Leslie, *Kohima: The Furthest Battle* (2009)
Graham, Gordon, *The Trees Are All Young on Garrison Hill* (2005)
Havers, Norman, *March On* (1992)
Keane, Feargal, *Road of Bones* (2010)
Kirby, S. Woodburn, *The War Against Japan* (5 volumes, HMSO, 1957–61)
Lucas-Philips, C.E., *Springboard to Victory* (1966)
Lyman, Robert, *Kohima 1944: The Battle that Saved India* (2010)
Slim, Field Marshal William, *Defeat into Victory* (1958)
Thompson, Julian, *Forgotten Voices of Burma* (2009)

INDEX

EXPLORE HISTORY'S MAJOR CONFLICTS WITH
BATTLE STORY

978-0-7524-6196-0

978-0-7524-6310-0

978-0-7524-8870-7

978-0-7524-6878-5

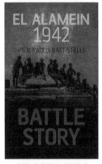

978-0-7524-6202-8

978-0-7524-7956-9

978-0-7524-8056-5

978-0-7524-6311-7

978-0-7524-6576-0

Visit our website and discover thousands of
other History Press books.
www.thehistorypress.co.uk